AMERICAN HERITAGE
ILLUSTRATED HISTORY
OF THE UNITED STATES

The Arch Street Ferry in Philadelphia as engraved by William and Thomas Birch.
FREE LIBRARY OF PHILADELPHIA

FRONT COVER: *Detail of a painting of the Constitutional Convention, held in Philadelphia on May 25, 1787.*
INDEPENDENCE NATIONAL HISTORICAL PARK COLLECTION, PHILADELPHIA

FRONT ENDSHEET: *Washington reviews troops called to put down the Whiskey Rebellion in 1794, when Pennsylvania farmers rioted over a tax on liquor.*
EDGAR WILLIAM AND BERNICE CHRYSLER GARBISCH COLLECTION, NATIONAL GALLERY OF ART

CONTENTS PAGE: *American naval uniforms were dressier in 1812 than today.*
NEW YORK HISTORICAL SOCIETY

BACK ENDSHEET: *The Battle of New Orleans, as drawn on the field by an American army engineer, was fought two weeks after peace was signed. The British lost more than 2,000, including three generals. The Americans lost only 71.*
MABEL BRADY GARVAN COLLECTION, YALE UNIVERSITY ART GALLERY

BACK COVER: *The Stars and Stripes that flew over Fort McHenry (top left); Thomas Jefferson, as painted by Rembrandt Peale in 1805 (top right); The Battle of New Orleans (bottom), a key American victory in the War of 1812.*
THE SMITHSONIAN INSTITUTE; NEW YORK HISTORICAL SOCIETY

AMERICAN HERITAGE ILLUSTRATED HISTORY OF THE UNITED STATES

VOLUME 4

A NEW NATION

BY ROBERT G. ATHEARN

Created in Association with the
Editors of AMERICAN HERITAGE

and for the updated edition
MEDIA PROJECTS INCORPORATED

CHOICE PUBLISHING, INC.
New York

Library of Congress Catalog Card Number: 87-73399
ISBN 0-945260-12-1
ISBN 0-945260-00-8

This 1988 edition is published and distributed by Choice Publishing, Inc., 53 Watermill Lane, Great Neck, NY 11021
by arrangement with American Heritage, a division of Forbes, Inc.

Manufactured in the United States of America
10 9 8 7 6 5 4 3

CONTENTS OF THE COMPLETE SERIES

Editor's Note to the Revised Edition
Introduction by ALLAN NEVINS
Main text by ROBERT G. ATHEARN

EACH VOLUME CONTAINS AN ENCYCLOPEDIC SECTION; MASTER INDEX IN VOLUME 18

CONTENTS OF VOLUME 4

CHAPTER 10

MEN AND OPPORTUNITY

It is a difficult thing to see one age through the eyes of another, to hear with it, feel with it, think with it, and to grasp the spirit of other times. Yet those who study the record of the American Revolution and the years immediately following it cannot escape the conclusion that this was, for all its struggle, one of the great periods of history in which to be alive.

To the former colonists themselves —and even more so to Europeans—it was astonishing that in seven years they could actually achieve the life and liberty they had proclaimed. Would they now also succeed in that even more difficult quest—the "pursuit of happiness"?

The 18th century, that era of enlightenment which liked to call itself the Age of Reason, looked hopefully to the American Republic. Europe had come to know the eminent Dr. Franklin—scientist, wit, philosopher, and democrat; if the other Americans were like him, then the future of his country was promising. Perhaps the

Portraits of Madison, Jay, and Hamilton surround manuscript, newspaper, and book copies of the Federalist essays they wrote.

New World would at last achieve and make into law the "rights of man" about which men had argued so long. These sturdy farmers called to mind the Romans in the days of the Republic. Unlike jaded Europe, they had no mob, no nobles, no king. Indeed, their great General Washington, like Cincinnatus 2,000 years before, had laid down his sword, bowed to the Congress, and returned to his farm, a hero out of Plutarch.

This was, perhaps, a sentimental picture, but it was true that the leaders of America had classic models, Greek and Roman, before their eyes as they set to organizing their new life as freemen. They were, unlike so many revolutionists before and afterward, well-educated and open-minded believers in "natural law"—a kind of common-sense set of universal rules made by the Creator, under which men had innate title to civil liberties, to popular sovereignty, and to the right of revolt. They owed, they felt, nothing to the past, which Washington called "a gloomy age of ignorance and superstition."

The war had brought forward many talented men, and now these same

275

young public figures, uplifted by the sense that they lived in a climactic moment of history, proved themselves great. Alexander Hamilton, Thomas Jefferson, James Madison, John Marshall, John Adams, John Dickinson, George Mason, and a dozen more—these Founding Fathers stare down at us stiffly like old men in their formal portraits, all ruffles and high collars and powdered wigs, but they were very much alive in those days. Never has a young nation been so richly endowed with vigorous leaders.

A raw new country

Nor has a country been so in need of them. Excepting only the un-counted Indians, scarcely 3,000,000 people lived in the new states, and all but a handful of them lived in the country. Philadelphia, the largest city, had 40,000 inhabitants. New York had 30,000, Boston 20,000. Most people clung to the seaboard, or lived near tidewater on which they could travel and ship their goods, for roads were primitive and slow. Even between Boston and New York, served by a stagecoach three times a week, the trip took three jogging, bouncing, uncomfortable days. It was two more days to Philadelphia. In the South there were no roads or stages at all, and the traveler went on horseback, following paths and trails. Of necessity, the states lived separate and apart on the civilized edge of a continent no one had crossed. Behind the coastal fringe lay the still-untamed Alleghenies, and

beyond them a few frontier settlements dotted the vast Northwest Territory, today's Middle West, which the United States had acquired from England in the peace settlement.

The vast majority of the people lived by a primitive agriculture. There were no factories, for the Industrial Revolution still lay in the future. Almost all the necessities of life were made at home, and the typical farmer supported his family by means and methods that had seen little change in a thousand years. The only power was supplied by animals, wind and water, and human muscle. It was a hard, if often rewarding, life, and even then not all the 3,000,000 quite lived up to the hopeful visions of the faraway philosophers in Paris: Six hundred thousand of the Americans were slaves, most but not all of them in the South. Three hundred thousand of the white men were not free either, but bound to service for some period of time as indentured servants, in payment of their passage to America. Of the rest, fully half were women who had no voting rights, and even among the freemen who made up the balance, perhaps only about 120,000 could meet all the property, religious, and other requirements for the franchise in the several states. Although the United States was a middle-class nation and had general social democracy as it began its experiment with political liberty, it was neither united nor democratic in its government, and it had need of all the brilliance that the Founding Fathers

The first American map of the United States, by Adam Buell in 1784, extends Connecticut, Virginia, the Carolinas, Georgia, Florida to the Mississippi.

could bring to bear on its many problems.

If the best government is the least government, as many philosophers have contended, the United States in 1783 had the world's finest. Certainly it had the least government of any civilized country. During the long

Lafayette visits George Washington and his family at Mount Vernon in 1784. The Frenchman idolized the American, even considering him his adoptive father.

war, the Continental Congress had, of course, done all within its power to manage the fighting and carry on a government. It had contracted offensive and defensive alliances, raised an army, tried to establish a navy, borrowed money, and issued currency, however unstable that currency turned out to be. Its only authority was necessity, and its few commands, therefore, had been generally accepted.

A formal instrument of government had indeed been proposed in 1776, by the same Richard Henry Lee who had offered the resolution for independence. His Articles of Confederation were adopted in 1777, but did not come into effect—fortunately, perhaps—until 1781, when the war was all but over. For they weakened even further the power of the central government, which, as Washington observed in dismay, was "a half-starved, limping" thing, unable to govern or restrain the states. The Congress, said Dr. Benjamin Rush of Philadelphia, was "abused, laughed at, and cursed in every company." In fact, in June, 1783, when a group of disgruntled and threatening veterans marched on Philadelphia to demand their back pay, Congress had to flee to Princeton, New Jersey, penniless and abject. Was poor old George III so wrong when he observed more in sorrow than in

anger that the United States "certainly for many years cannot have any stable government"?

Family quarrels

Even before the war was safely won, there were enough squabbles among the states to suggest that the king might be right. One state, for example, would arouse the animosity of the others by refusing to obey the requisitions of Congress. Neighboring states would battle over boundaries,

and there were countless arguments about trade regulations. Such wrangling not only embarrassed the central government, but was unnecessarily hard on foreign commercial houses. European nations naturally shied away from trade treaties with a country so weak and divided. From the outset, the credit rating of the United States was poor.

Rivalry was intense among the major seaports. In the lower South, most imports entered at Charleston; in the upper South, at Baltimore. The middle states received their foreign goods at either Philadelphia or New York, and New England at Boston. Immediately after the war, most of the states placed revenue-raising tariffs on imports. New England and the middle states, in particular, were developing home industries, and here tariffs were intended to protect them. The South, having no promising manufacturing, held its rates low, hoping to keep down the prices of goods its

279

people bought. Southerners fumed at New England as a result.

On their part, the small New England states were bitter about the money New York made by virtue of its superior port facilities. Many of the articles used in Connecticut, New Jersey, Vermont, and western Massachusetts were bought in New York. Tariff revenues were of course added to the price. Unhappy residents of Connecticut claimed they paid an annual toll of 50,000 pounds into the New York treasury. New Jersey merchants were especially unhappy over the situation, and called for some centralized government power that would protect the little states. Matters got even worse when in 1787 the New York legislature decided to collect entrance and clearance fees from vessels trading with such foreign lands as New Jersey and Connecticut.

The 13 independent Americas

Because the states were long used to trading with the British, they naturally tried to continue. In 1785, John

When the Massachusetts legislature refused to aid the farmers, they rebelled in 1786 under Daniel Shays, attacking officials and the Springfield arsenal.

280

Adams went to London as the first official American minister, seeking to re-establish a healthy commerce. The king received him politely, but the British foreign minister was not quite so agreeable. Adams was advised that if the United States wished to make a trade treaty, *they* ought properly to. send over 13 representatives, as there was no sign of unity at home.

In the eyes of the British, our new government was guilty of a kind of bad faith, for Congress could not persuade the quarreling states even to live up to the peace treaty signed by their representatives. In it, America had promised creditors on each side that they would not be prevented from collecting their lawful debts at full sterling value. It had also agreed to urge upon the state legislatures the necessity of returning confiscated estates taken from British subjects. Loyalists who had fought for England, many of them now penniless and desperate, were to be granted a full year to go anywhere in the United States and press for the return of their property. The treaty had further stated there would be no more confiscations.

When the states learned that Congress had made such promises, they objected vigorously. Nevertheless, in January, 1784, Congress issued a proclamation asking all states holding property taken from the loyalists to return it. Fearing unrest and possibly riots if they tried to carry out the request, the state legislatures did not hurry to comply. It is not one of the brightest pages in our history. In almost every state there were violations of the Treaty of 1783. Southerners were more inclined than Northerners to ignore Congress, for the British had carried off or freed many slaves without bothering to pay.

Time would heal the raw wounds of war, and the day would come when America's pledged word would be accepted, but the British were in no mood to wait for history; few creditors are. They applied pressure. By 1785, two years after the peace terms were signed, the United States learned that the British had no intention of evacuating their garrisons at Oswego, Niagara, Detroit, and other places until such offenders as New York and Virginia repealed some of their antiloyalist legislation. Even though men like Alexander Hamilton, George Washington, James Monroe, and John Marshall threw all their personal influence into the fight for compliance to treaty terms from their states, they were rebuffed, and the reputation of the Confederation government sank to a new low. Separatists were thriving, and a State of Franklin was actually set up, from 1784 to 1788, in western North Carolina. The Northwest was slipping away. Debts were mounting. Would the Confederation hold together?

Demands for a change

By 1787, Congress had failed so consistently to govern that it was held in almost no respect. Since the Revo-

When the Constitutional Convention, under Washington's leadership, met on May 25, 1787, at Independence Hall, the assemblage included most of the important American political leaders of the day.

lution, the quality of its membership had declined as each state persuaded its ablest leaders to stay in local positions.

So low had the interest in Congress sunk that that body could not even get the necessary quorum of nine states. From October, 1785, until April, 1786, there were only three days when enough members were present to conduct business. There was no money to pay civil officials or soldiers, and soldiers had mutinied. Money borrowed from Europe was exhausted, and American representatives abroad could not collect their salaries. There was ominous talk of establishing a monarchy, and many who abhorred the idea were forced to conclude that it was the only defense against chaos. George Washington saw that some drastic step was necessary when he wrote, "I do not conceive we can exist long as a nation without having lodged somewhere a power, which will pervade the whole Union in as energetic a manner as the authority of the State government extends over the several States."

Other thinking men also decided it was time for a change. As early as 1780, Alexander Hamilton, then only 23, declared that if Congress did not assume dictatorial powers, a general convention should be called. At his urging, the New York legislature later proposed such a meeting to amend the Articles of Confederation.

In 1785, Governor James Bowdoin of Massachusetts tried to hasten the movement for stronger central government when he recommended to his legislature the necessity of a convention. The legislators responded by asking Congress to call the states together. Unhappily, the course of state sovereignty was running at flood tide, and the Massachusetts delegates in Congress took it upon themselves to withhold the request. They asked the governor if this was not too bold a move. Perhaps they agreed with Jef-

INDEPENDENCE NATIONAL HISTORICAL PARK, PHILADELPHIA

ferson, then far away as the American minister at Paris, who wrote that he liked "a little rebellion now and then" and who wondered if the Indians, who had no central government at all, were not the best off.

By 1786, the independent spirit was running rampant throughout the states. In New Hampshire, mobs demanding a distribution of property and paper money rioted outside the building while legislators met. Rhode Island merchants were so hard-pressed by a law obliging them to accept payment in scrip that they closed their shops. Nearby, in Massachusetts, there was a frightening farmers' uprising. By 1785, their state taxes had risen to about a third of their income, which had to be paid in specie—hard money —something rarely seen on a farm. In 1786, taxes were raised again, the legislature refused to print cheap paper money, and debt-ridden farmers began to be evicted from their property by the courts. Daniel Shays, once a captain in the Revolution, and a band of 500 desperate men forced one court to close after facing down the state militia. Later, leading 1,200 men, he tried to seize the arsenal at Springfield and was routed only by gunfire.

It was a commercial question that finally prompted action. Maryland and Virginia fell to bickering over navigational rights on the Potomac

River, but agreed to discussion at Washington's Mount Vernon home. So successful were the talks that when Maryland suggested enlarging the agreements, the idea met with favor. Both Pennsylvania and Delaware showed interest, as did men like Hamilton and Madison, who had already been hard at work on proposed government reforms, and they took the necessary step of inviting all the states to a general trade convention. The meeting was arranged for September, 1786; the place, Annapolis. Although only five states actually sent delegates, Alexander Hamilton, representing New York and eager to use almost any device to strengthen the national government, managed to arrange another meeting—an all-important one as it turned out—at Philadelphia in May, 1787. James Madison assisted him. Congress cooperated by issuing the call, but specified that the meeting was to be for the sole purpose of revising the Articles of Confederation.

Hidden strengths of the Confederation

Although it unconsciously signed its own death warrant by agreeing to the Philadelphia convention, the old Confederation could nevertheless look back on a few achievements. During its later years, which historian John Fiske called the "critical period," it had provided the new nation with a greater sense of direction than many realized. Legend has it that Fisher Ames, soon to be a Congressman from Massachusetts, provided a pop-

At the Constitutional Convention, Edmund Randolph proposed the controversial Virginia Plan.

ular description of this new democracy. Monarchy, he said, is like a full-rigged ship, trim and beautiful, with all hands at their stations and the captain at the helm. It executes its maneuvers sharply and operates with the greatest efficiency, but if it hits a rock, the frail hull is crushed and the vessel sinks. Democracy is like a raft—hard to navigate, impossible to keep on course, and distressingly slow. If it runs onto a rock, it simply careens off and takes a new course. But if it has the virtue of always staying afloat, it has disadvantages, too. As Ames said, "Damn it, your feet are wet all the time."

Men who were distressed over the weakness of the Confederation government were more worried about wet feet than about the progress they had made, unnoticed. During its short history that government had formulated two of the most vital pieces of legislation in the history of the United States. The first was the farseeing Ordinance of 1785, which set forth the fundamentals of our land system and provided a pattern for the future.

This thoughtful law provided for a survey of Western lands, the property of the central government, into rectangular townships of 36 square miles each. Each square mile was called a section, and it contained 640 acres, sold for $1 each. By means of the advance survey, the government was able to mark off its salable land on maps and issue titles with more efficiency and equity. Although many sections fell into the hands of speculators and land companies, the survey still leaves its mark. Anyone flying across the nation today can observe the checkerboard result. Evidence that the young government was interested in education may be found in the fact that one section in every township was reserved for schools.

The Northwest Ordinance of 1787, the Confederation's second great piece of legislation, provided for the political subdivision of the territory north and west of the Ohio River known as the Northwest Territory. Slavery was to be excluded. By that law, a governor, a secretary, and three judges were appointed. When any of the territories laid out in that area contained 5,000 adult males, the people were to have a two-chamber legislature and a voice in their own government. When its free inhabitants reached 60,000, a territory might apply for statehood and attain equal standing with the other states. This was the direct opposite of the old European system; the states would have no colonies and only equal sisters. Daniel Webster later said that he doubted "whether one single law of any lawgiver, ancient or modern, has produced effects of more distinct, marked, and lasting character than the Ordinance of 1787."

Drawing up a new set of rules

The convention date had been set for May 14, 1787, but bad weather and worse roads delayed the arrival of a number of delegates. On May 25, a quorum of seven states was finally on hand. (New Hampshire was the last to arrive—over two months late—and Rhode Island never sent representatives at all.) Once the sessions began—at the old Pennsylvania State House, later known as Independence Hall with George Washington presiding—problems were attacked in earnest. To insure quiet in that era of cobblestones and noisy iron-rimmed wagon wheels, the streets in front of the building were muffled by spreading loose dirt. Public interest was great. Well-known figures like James Madison and Edmund Randolph of Virginia, Gouverneur Morris and Benjamin Franklin of Pennsylvania, and Rufus King of Massachusetts gathered at the sessions, and in off hours at the Indian Queen Tavern, to lend their talents to the work. The delegates ranged in age from Dr. Franklin, who was 81, to Jonathan Dayton of New Jersey, who was only 26. Jefferson, who was not present, was so impressed by their qualities that he referred to the meeting as "an assembly of demigods."

The leaders among the 55 delegates were ready for a bold step. They decided to ignore the instructions that they do nothing but amend the Articles of Confederation. Although the Confederation Congress was sitting nearby, working out the measures of the Northwest Ordinance, they resolved to devise a new form of government. To keep their proceedings secret, they posted sentries at the doors. For the same reason, few records were kept, and we owe our knowledge of the debates mainly to notes kept by James Madison, which were not published until more than half a century later, four years after his death.

At the start, Edmund Randolph of Virginia stepped forward with a plan named after his state. It proposed a two-house national legislature with the power to do all those things with respect to taxation, commerce, finance, war, and treaty making in which the old system had proved itself so weak. Under the Virginia Plan, the lower house would be elected by the people, and the upper house would be chosen by the lower from nominees of the state legislatures. The Virginians could observe, along with the new state governments, the English Parliament with its House of Lords and its House of Commons acting as a check upon each other—the hereditary Lords conservative and free from fickle popular favor, and the elected Commons (for all its faults in that era) the more representative voice of the people, with, in effect, the power to give money to the executive or withhold it from him. Randolph's plan also proposed an executive chosen by the legislature, a judiciary including a supreme court and lower courts, and a council of revision made up of the executive and several members of the judiciary with a veto power over the legislature.

There was much opposition to one point or another of the Virginia Plan, but most of it was centered around the fact that both houses of the legislature would be chosen on a basis of population. The small states were displeased because this meant they would have much less power than their heavily populated neighbors like Virginia and New York. And so the Virginia Plan was countered by a New Jersey Plan, representing the views of the small states. It returned to the idea of a single legislature, with one vote for every state, a plural executive with less power, and a supreme court. In essence it was the Articles of Confederation again, but with much greater power given to Congress. It also proposed to levy taxes on a basis proportionate to population, counting whites in full, slaves at three-fifths, and no Indians—a device that eventually carried

George Mason (left), a delegate to the Constitutional Convention from Virginia, and Elbridge Gerry (center) from Massachusetts refused to sign its final document. William Paterson countered the Virginia Plan with the New Jersey Plan.

over into the Constitution.

The argument was solved at last, as most are, by a compromise. Roger Sherman of Connecticut proposed that membership in the lower house be allotted in proportion to population, but that each state be equal in the other house, with one vote. The proposal was modified in the great debate that followed, but Sherman's suggestion paved the way to agreement and gave the country the House and Senate as they exist today.

When they came to provide an executive, the delegates turned away after a while from the notion of having this person (or persons) elected by Congress; they believed that dependence on the favor of an all-powerful legislature would weaken him too much. Only a few favored popular election—among them Dr. Franklin, John Dickinson, Gouverneur Morris,

and James Wilson. But most delegates felt that the people were simply not up to such a responsibility. They were not "sufficiently informed," thought Roger Sherman. Asking the people to pick a good executive was like referring "a trial of colors to a blind man," remarked George Mason.

The eventual compromise on this question was the work of Morris and Madison, who put forward an adaptation of the method used by Maryland in choosing its state senators—a body of electors. Each of the states, they suggested, would have as many electors as it had Representatives and Senators in Congress, appointed "in such manner as the legislature thereof may direct." This was indirect election. When the "electoral college" then voted for a President, it would elect the candidate who received a majority of the votes of all the electors. The

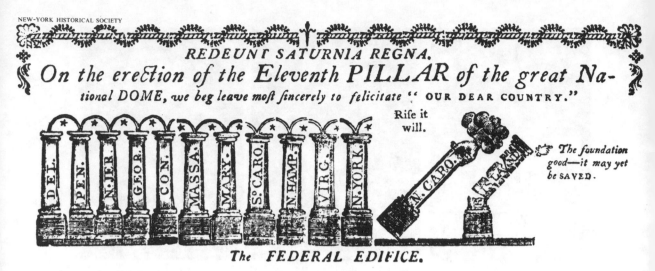

REDEUNT SATURNIA REGNA.

On the erection of the Eleventh PILLAR of the great National DOME, we beg leave most sincerely to felicitate " OUR DEAR COUNTRY."

Rise it will.

☞ *The foundation good—it may yet be SAVED.*

The FEDERAL EDIFICE.

When the 11th state—powerful New York—ratified, the Constitution was considered nationally acceptable, even without North Carolina and Rhode Island.

runner-up would be Vice-President (although this was altered later). Even that leading conservative Alexander Hamilton, who had hoped for a life-time executive, or "Governor," of the United States (with power to appoint state governors!), was satisfied with this solution. He was sure it would prevent any "cabal, intrigue, and corruption." Everyone assumed that the electors under this system would be the cream of American society, fiercely independent, pledged to no one person, and that they would consider long and carefully, often weighing many candidates, before choosing one to fill four years in the exalted office. What in fact has happened to the electoral college is well known, but it was not foreseen at that time. And as the delegates had that model of honor and rectitude, General Washington, in mind for the first President, they agreed to the electoral plan.

The one fact that stands out clearly in a document referred to as a "bundle of compromises" is the notion of the separation of powers. The states delegated some and kept others. Each of the three branches of the central government—legislative, executive, and judicial—was provided with the power to check the others. Congress could exercise a measure of control over the judiciary through its appointive power. The executive could veto an act of Congress, but that body in turn could override the veto. And, finally, the Supreme Court might declare unauthorized acts of Congress unconstitutional. As became apparent later, the most important question not answered was whether a state might withdraw—that is, secede—from the new Union.

When enough compromises had been made to reassure the delegates who were most fearful, the document was ready for signing. Then it came out that all the repairing and patching had produced a result unsatisfactory to other members. George Mason, Elbridge Gerry, and Edmund Randolph flatly refused to sign. Washington, Franklin, and Hamilton had reservations but, feeling that progress had been made, gave their approval. A man living in Philadelphia at the time of the convention later said that talks with various delegates had convinced him that no one of them was wholly satisfied.

Those who gathered at Philadelphia that summer of 1787 accomplished much more than they realized. Casting aside the relatively weak Articles of Confederation, whose only strength was based upon the willingness of individual states to cooperate, they forged a new instrument of great potential power. Inherent in the Constitution was the notion that sovereignty lay with individuals, not with state governments. The idea of democratic republics was not new, but in the European models, the component parts (or political subdivisions) contributed the power. In the new American Republic, both the states and the central government drew their authority from the same source—the people. And the people were citizens both of their home states and of the nation. By their actions the framers of the Constitution spread the national government's jurisdiction across the face of the nation, and for the first time made it possible for voters to decide upon purely national issues. They may not have regarded their work as revolutionary, as most of their ideas were drawn from earlier colonial experience, but the long-range result was to be far from conservative in its nature. As Madison commented, they had "built for the ages," and it was true. No other nation in the modern world is still governed by so ancient and durable an instrument. Yet, ironically enough, it would probably never have been adopted if there could, in that era, have been a popular vote.

The campaign for ratification

Although still having some doubts about the nature of their work, the delegates bravely presented it to their fellow Americans for approval. Trying to cover up their own disagreements, they said at the end of the Constitution that it was "done in convention by the unanimous consent of the states present," and the approval of ratifying conventions in nine states was required to make it binding. Pennsylvania at once called a convention, but it was beaten by Delaware. The little state, eager to benefit by the guarantees offered, became the first to ratify, in early December. A few days later another small state, New Jersey, went along. In January, 1788, Georgia and Connecticut followed. Not all of the smaller states were so enthusiastic. Rhode Island stood aloof and stoutly refused to join her sisters. Proponents of the new government were of course discouraged by this attitude, but then the important state of Massachusetts voted yes, 187 to 168. Although the Massachusetts majority was small, six states had now approved.

During the spring of 1788, victory for the Constitution makers was assured. Maryland and South Carolina ratified in April, New Hampshire and Virginia in June. The contest in Virginia was particularly violent, with the fiery Patrick Henry and the well-known Richard Henry Lee leading the opposition. They feared the loss of state power to the young giant spawned at Philadelphia. Only the persuasive powers of respected figures like Washington, Madison, and Marshall tipped the scales against them.

In New York the battle was no less spectacular. The seaboard merchants, who saw commercial stability stemming from a strong central government, favored the change. But the upcountry farmers, jealous of their local rights and fearful of the merchant class, opposed it with all their strength. Hamilton and John Jay worked tirelessly to win them over. James Madison of Virginia helped them out when he joined in their propaganda campaign. The essays they produced are today known as *The Federalist*. They first appeared, hopefully to influence the whole country, immediately after the Constitutional Convention adjourned and before any ratifying convention met. They were widely printed by newspapers. Without them we would know much less about the origins of our government.

By midsummer of 1788, 11 of the 13 states had approved the Constitution. Two held out—but not for long. North Carolina ratified in 1789, and Rhode Island in May, 1790.

The Americans choose up sides

One of the fundamental rights claimed by Americans, from earliest colonial times, was that of dissent. They recognized that there were two sides—at least—to every question and felt that nothing was so healthy as the airing of opposing views. Just as the men who wrote the Constitution debated, so did the American people. Except in some of the smaller states, which were happy to join the Union for its benefits, the debate was long and difficult.

Great issues oblige men to take sides. The contest over ratification divided the nation into those for and those against. Up to this time we had no political parties, but out of this debate there arose the Federalist and Antifederalist groups, which would soon resolve themselves into political organizations with causes of their own. Although the Constitution makers envisaged no such development, the document itself produced a division, and the two-party system was born.

For the moment, however, party politics were submerged. The eyes of the nation turned to the Virginian, George Washington, and for the only time in American history a President was elected without any competition.

THOMAS JEFFERSON

Thomas Jefferson made a great personal contribution to the United States. All his life he had his vision of what this country should be, and he did everything he could to make this vision a reality. He foresaw a United States with a democratic, representative government—one that placed much of the responsibility on the individual and relied little on strong central control. He eloquently set forth his ideas about government in the Declaration of Independence. He continued to advance them in every public post he held. Jefferson also had a vision of his country stretching across the continent. With his encouragement of the Lewis and Clark explorations and his purchase of Louisiana in 1803, he did much to make this dream come true. He took great interest in the kind of education Americans would have, the architecture of the buildings they would erect, and even in what they would grow in their gardens and orchards. He was never a casual bystander. Jefferson was deeply involved in every aspect of American life, and in this involvement lay his greatness.

THOMAS JEFFERSON

JEFFERSON THE RADICAL

MAD TOM in A RAGE

Thomas Jefferson was always a controversial figure. His forcefully democratic ideas as second governor of Virginia (1779–81) were considered radical by many. But Jefferson felt he was only living up to Virginia's revolutionary spirit as expressed on its first state seal above, where Virtue triumphs over the fallen figure of Tyranny bereft of his crown. When Jefferson was inaugurated third President of the United States in 1801, he was no less controversial. The Federalist cartoon at the left supposedly shows Jefferson, referred to as Mad Tom, attempting to pull down the federal government with assistance from the Devil. Such fears stemmed from Jefferson's vigorously expressed sentiments against a strong national government. There was even more headshaking when he bought the huge Louisiana Territory from France, a purchase that more than doubled the size of the United States. New Orleans' historic Place d'Armes (right) was the scene of impressive ceremonies in 1803 as the French tricolor was replaced by the American flag and the United States took possession of what it had bought.

THE ARCHITECT

Jefferson's energy and talent were boundless. He was a fine architect in the classical tradition. The single building that most influenced his ideas about architecture was the Maison Carree, a Roman ruin in Nimes, France (opposite). He considered it the finest remaining example of classical design. Its lines are mirrored in his own work, especially in the state capitol he designed for Virginia. It still stands in Richmond, and one of the first models of it is seen at the left. Jefferson's last great project was designing the buildings for the University of Virginia in Charlottesville. The 1824 engraving above shows the campus dominated by the great rotunda. Its dome, also typical of Jefferson's style, was inspired by the famous Halle aux Bles in Paris.

VIRGINIA STATE CAPITOL

294

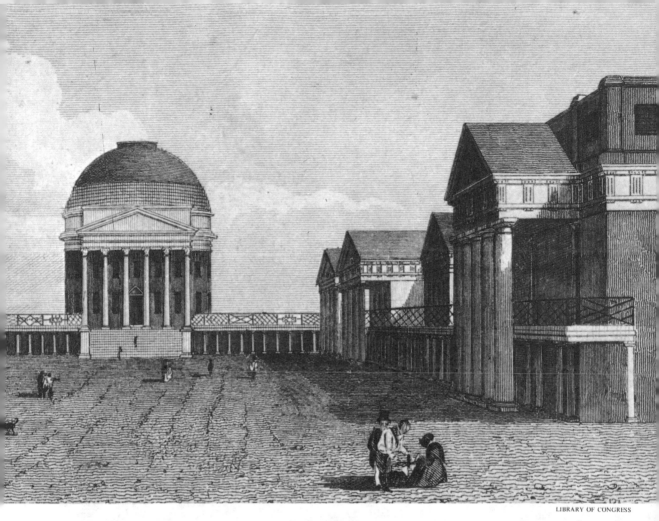

THE LOUVRE, PARIS

THOMAS JEFFERSON

MR. MAMMOTH

When he was a boy, Thomas Jefferson collected Indian artifacts. As a man, he remained interested in every aspect of natural history—even paleontology, for which his enemies derisively nicknamed him Mr. Mammoth. He was head of the American Philosophical Society, which, in 1801, financed the excavation of the bones of a prehistoric mastodon in New York. Below is the scene painted by Charles Willson Peale, who also belonged to the society. In the portrait opposite, Caleb Boyle painted Jefferson before Virginia's Natural Bridge, which he once owned.

THOMAS JEFFERSON

THE INVENTOR

Jefferson leveled a mountaintop near Charlottesville for Monticello. The cottage (right) where he brought his bride in 1772 was the first part to be built. It was connected to the main house by a semisubterranean series of servants' quarters and kitchens. His law office (left) was connected by a row of stables. At Monticello, Jefferson showed his inventiveness. On his travels he noted anything that made life easier, often adapted it for his own use. A fireplace concealed a dumbwaiter, which brought up wine bottles from the cellar. A quartet stand was devised to hold the music for four musicians. (Jefferson was an enthusiastic violinist.) A polygraph was designed to cut down writing time. As Jefferson wrote with one pen, another made a copy. He wrote more than 25,000 letters.

299

FEDERAL HALL

The Seat of Congress

er Lacour delin.

A. Doolittle Scu

CHAPTER 11

WASHINGTON AT THE HELM

In the years since his death, the figure of George Washington—brave, wise, upright—has gradually been turned into a marble statue, as if he had no feelings and never suffered doubt. But turn to his diary for April 16, 1789, as he prepared to assume the first Presidency of the United States under the Constitution:

About 10 o'clock I bade farewell to Mount Vernon, to private life, and to domestic felicity; and with a mind oppressed with more anxious and painful sensations than I have words to express, set out for New York.

The man who had been unanimously chosen for his great office, the man whose calmness, dignity, and strength everyone relied upon to steer the fragile new ship of state, had to borrow money for the trip! Like his country, he had land aplenty, and little cash.

By April 23, he had arrived in New York, which was to serve as the capital for a year until the government would move to Philadelphia. (Gloomy

Washington's first inauguration took place on the balcony of Federal Hall in New York, then the government's capital.

New Yorkers predicted that thereafter their city would become deserted, "a wilderness, peopled with wolves.") As great crowds gathered on April 30 at Federal Hall in Wall Street, Washington made his way to its balcony "accompanied," he said, "by feelings not unlike those of a culprit, who is going to the place of his execution." His voice was low, his manner grave. For the occasion he wore a simple brown suit, woven of 100% American homespun, and only a plain sword to recall the military man—as if to bear witness that this would be a country ruled by civilians. Then he was sworn in by Robert R. Livingston, chancellor of the State of New York, and stepped back inside to address the dignitaries in the Senate chamber.

Much the same group who struggled and fought over the new Constitution at Philadelphia was now on hand in the various branches of the government, united by the desire to make it work, but by little else. There was John Adams, the first Vice-President, founder of a brilliant Massachusetts dynasty, intelligent and honorable, but so pompous in his new dignity that scoffers fell to calling him

This fanciful painting of Washington's arrival in New York for his inauguration presents an image more suitable to King Arthur than life in 18th-century America.

His Rotundity. He was scarcely what we would today call a democrat. "The proposition that the people are the best keepers of their own liberties," he observed, "is not true." There was brilliant John Jay of New York, soon to be the first Chief Justice. His view? "Those who own the country ought to govern it."

And there was one small, dapper, bright-eyed, and handsome man, intensely ambitious—more, perhaps, for his country than himself. This was Washington's former aide and chief author of *The Federalist,* Alexander Hamilton, who had been chosen Secretary of the Treasury. Here are some of his views, for the glimpse they give of how times have changed since 1789:

> *All communities divide themselves into the few and the many. The first are rich and wellborn, the other the mass of the people. The voice of the people has been said to be the voice of God; and however generally this maxim has been quoted and believed, it is not true in fact. The people are turbulent and changing; they seldom judge or determine right. Give therefore to the first class a distinct, permanent share in the government. They will check the unsteadiness of the second.*

But there were other views represented in this remarkable company. There was James Madison of Virginia, advocate of religious liberty, the man who would introduce the Bill of Rights into the Constitution, of which he was the leading author. And there was, above all, that paladin of the rights of man, Thomas Jefferson, the well-bred Virginian who believed in the perfectibility of the "second class" to whom Hamilton referred. In his mind, the ideal society would be an

agrarian republic founded on equality among individual freeholders. He distrusted the cities and the threat of organized finance. He feared powerful industry and a strong central government. It was inevitable that Jefferson would clash with Hamilton, although this was not immediately apparent in the first days of the first administration under the new Constitution.

Unlike any President since his time, Washington did not inherit an already operating machine. Instead, everything had to be created, or done, or even thought of for the first time. There was much to consider as the

303

first Congress began its deliberations. It had to organize itself and provide its own rules. One of the first tasks was the preparation and submission to the various states of the first 10 amendments to the Constitution—the Bill of Rights, urged by Madison. These protections of individual liberty had been demanded by five state ratifying conventions and pledged by Federalist leaders. By December 15, 1791, they had become part of the Constitution.

It was also necessary to provide for the judiciary called for in the charter, including the Supreme Court and the lower courts. As first Chief Justice, Washington appointed a New Yorker, John Jay, and to operate the law enforcement machinery, such as it was, he appointed Edmund Randolph as Attorney General. Departments of War, Treasury, Post Office, and State were also set up, making a cabinet of five. As Secretary of War, Washington appointed his portly and faithful friend, General Henry Knox of Massachusetts; as Secretary of the Treasury, Alexander Hamilton; as Postmaster General, Samuel Osgood, who had commanded a company of minutemen at Lexington; and as Secretary of State, Thomas Jefferson. Although Jefferson had not taken an active part in the work on the Constitution, and was philosophically at odds with Hamilton, Washington trusted him as a friend and neighbor, respected his brilliance and his experience abroad, and felt also that he should strive to

have all viewpoints represented in the administration.

One of the first problems facing the new management was the age-old matter of money. The government was in debt at birth to the extent of about $80,000,000, if foreign, domestic, and state debts were all counted. Daily expenses had begun on March 4, 1789—a provision made by the old Congress in the fall of 1788. Just as soon as the new Representatives took their oaths of office and prepared to function as a body, James Madison introduced the depressing subject. He asked for a temporary tariff law that would raise enough revenue to carry on government functions until a more permanent solution could be found.

Speculators, bootleggers, and finance

A tariff provided only for day-to-day expenses, however. Long-range plans were essential, and Alexander Hamilton now made a series of broad financial proposals aimed at putting the young nation on a more solid footing. Before the federal government's first birthday, he advocated funding the entire foreign and domestic debt into a single obligation. To raise the necessary money, new securities would be offered for sale. His plan was to assume all American obligations, state and federal, from the beginning of the Revolution, at face value. It would still come to $80,000,-000, but the nation's credit abroad would be vastly improved.

The boldness of Hamilton's ap-

Alexander Hamilton, painted here by John Trumbull, was Washington's Secretary of the Treasury from 1789 to 1795, and spokesman for the Federalist Party.

proach aroused great controversy. Many government securities had depreciated heavily—for example, the scrip given to soldiers for their back pay, which was now selling at one-quarter of its face value. At once speculators raced out to the frontier with cash in their pockets, buying up these obligations cheaply from people who did not yet know that they could

soon collect in full. The speculators were, of course, delighted with Hamilton's plan. So also were those states with large debts that would be assumed by the central government. But states whose debts had been paid, or greatly reduced, objected to bailing out their more indigent sisters. Hamilton managed to have his way, but he had to turn to his opponents, Jefferson and Madison, for help. By means of an agreement whereby Virginia was promised Hamilton's support in getting the new capital city located on the Potomac, after 1800, the funding plan won enough Southern votes to squeak by.

Hamilton had just begun to fight. Next he asked for additional revenue to pay the interest on the obligations the government had assumed. He sought it through an excise tax to be laid on such homemade products as distilled liquors. The act passed in March, 1791, and before long the opposition grew so fierce, especially in western Pennsylvania, where tax money was scarce but distilling was a major industry, that Washington was obliged to call out troops in 1794 to put down what has been called the Whiskey Rebellion.

In a country with little cash, Hamilton was far-seeing enough to realize that a credit structure was needed, as it is in any modern state today. Debt —sound debt like federal bonds— is paradoxically the source of credit. Bonds make good paying investments, and bring wealth out of mattresses and strongboxes. Bonds can be borrowed against to provide capital, which starts factories and trade and creates more wealth. Consequently, Hamilton obviously had no intention of paying off his bond issues, which would have deflated the new economy. On the contrary, he sought to provide more credit, and machinery to operate it. Thus he turned to a British model, the Bank of England, and proposed to establish a national bank, supported

by both private and government funds. Jefferson fought this centralization with all his ability, charging that some members of the new government were "driving too fast," and that the Constitution had not mentioned any bank. Madison agreed with him and tried to stem the advance of national power as opposed to that of the states, but to no avail. The bill passed Congress, and President Washington signed it, after asking all his cabinet members their opinion. Hamilton argued most effectively. The Constitution, he said, gave Congress the right to regulate currency and trade, and this delegated power also implied the power to use any legitimate means, not specifically prohibited by the Constitution, to achieve that end. His interpretation is known as the "loose construction" theory of the Constitution, and Jefferson's as the "strict construction."

Hamilton followed his victories with more requests. In December, 1791, he made a report on manufacturing in which he presented a powerful argument for the protection of America's budding industries through tariffs and subsidies. More than a plan for merely fending off foreign competitors by means of a tariff, it antic-

HOWARD PYLE'S *Book of the American Spirit*, HARPER & ROW

Citizen Genet was sent by the French government in 1793 to get American aid, and although coolly received officially, he was eagerly entertained by the people.

ipated all kinds of improvements, ranging from an increased use of machinery to the encouragement of immigration as a source of labor.

In 1792, an act was passed that strengthened the existing tariffs and generally announced to the world that the government proposed to nurse its industrial fledglings. Hamilton had scored again and had given meaning to Pennsylvania Senator William Maclay's gloomy statement that "Congress may go home. Mr. Hamilton is all-powerful, and fails in nothing he attempts."

The crew divides

The Senator's statement was filled with significance. It put into words a sentiment that had already crossed many minds. During the early months of Washington's administration it was increasingly clear that his two assistants, Hamilton and Jefferson, were of divergent opinions in most matters. As the breach widened between them, their supporters, both in and out of Congress, took up the cause, and before the contest was over, America had two political parties, divided on many scores, personal and economic.

Even during the Constitutional Convention at Philadelphia, the merchant class had fought for the kind of government that would offer not only economic stability but specific encouragements to industry. In the Congressional debates over Hamilton's proposals, representatives of this same vocal, intelligent, hard-fighting group banded behind him, overeager to make secure the victory gained at Philadelphia. Because they stressed the need for a strong federal government, as opposed to an association of powerful individual states, they labeled themselves Federalists. President Washington, never formally a party man—indeed, an enemy of "factions"—nevertheless generally supported them more and more because they seemed practical.

Men of the opposition, who at first called themselves Antifederalists and later Democratic-Republicans, did not argue against the notion of national unity, although they wanted less of it, or at least a weaker central government. They agreed that the national debt should be honored, but they felt that Hamilton's plans tipped the scales in favor of merchants, bankers, and speculators. It appeared that the farmer and the planter were to be taxed, excessively they thought, only to aid bondholders and financiers in the cities. How, they asked, would a national bank assist ordinary countrymen? In short, they charged that the Federalists seemed to be running the government with class legislation.

Jefferson eloquently expressed the view of his followers that the Federalists were warping the Constitution and subverting the rights of the common man. The new government was riven by discord, and Massachusetts Representative Fisher Ames, a sharp-tongued Federalist who soon wearied of hearing his opponents cry "Unconstitutional," dashed off a few angry sentences that perhaps expressed the views of his colleagues: "I scarce know a point which has not produced this cry, not excepting a motion for adjournment. The fishery bill was unconstitutional; it was unconstitutional to receive plans of finance from the Secretary [of the Treasury]; to give bounties; to make the militia worth having; order is unconstitutional; credit is tenfold worse."

Another revolution affects America

If Washington's first administration rang with strife over taxes and finances, his second, to which he was again unanimously elected in 1792, suffered even greater struggles over foreign affairs. The successful Revolution in America had not gone unnoticed in Europe, especially in France, seething with poverty and discontent. Hardly had the new government set itself up in business in 1789 before the European continent was rocked by a revolution in France. The breadth of the Atlantic Ocean did not prevent Americans from taking an active interest; only recently the French had fought against England alongside Washington's army. When the hated Bastille fell in Paris and its worn prisoners streamed into the light, Lafayette sent its key to Washington as a token of revolutionary brotherhood.

As the French Revolution progressed, all followed its course with great interest, but, as was to be expected, there were two sharply divided camps—those who favored the revolutionaries and those who feared them. When the extremist Jacobins came to power, the king and queen were executed, and the guillotine began its long, bloody career under the detested Terror, the conservative Hamilton was appalled; Washington and the other Federalists were inclined to side with him. Jefferson, who had long known the French, took the other point of view. The professed ideals of the revolution were his, and, like many idealists in other times, he could not believe ill of it. He found support from Philip Freneau, editor of an American paper called the *National Gazette,* who used his columns as a mouthpiece for the Antifederalists. And so the two political parties, divided on domestic issues, were now also opposed in foreign affairs.

Differences of opinion over events in France were brought to a head in America by the arrival of a brilliant

"Mad Anthony" Wayne was ordered to avenge the massacre of settlers and soldiers in the Ohio country by Chief Little Turtle.

but unstable young Frenchman named Edmond Charles Genet, called Citizen Genet after the new French egalitarian fashion. He was appointed minister to the United States at the height of the revolutionary turmoil and sent with instructions that looked to embroiling this country in the war France had now declared on Great Britain, Spain, and Holland. Genet landed at Charleston on April 8, 1793, and began a leisurely trip toward Philadelphia. Like the Pied Piper of Hamelin, he fascinated the countryside as he progressed northward. It took him 28 days and an uncounted number of

Wayne routed the Indians in the Battle of Fallen Timbers in Ohio on August 20, 1794. After Little Turtle (center) surrendered, he signed a treaty that ceded southeastern Indiana and southern Ohio for about $9,500 in annuities.

banquets to get there. At the same time, he was abusing his position by trying to organize expeditions against Spanish and British territories, and by commissioning privateers to prey on British ships off American shores.

Meanwhile, Washington became alarmed at the extent of the sympathy for France and on April 22 issued a proclamation of neutrality. He did not use the word itself, but his talk of a "friendly and impartial" course toward the warring powers was enough to make Genet cancel impending testimonial dinners and make haste for Philadelphia, where Washington received him coolly. Jefferson and Madison, on the other hand, were delighted to meet the Frenchman, and he was so encouraged by their enthusiasm that he wrote home some rather extravagant reports of prospects on this side of the ocean. Presently, however, Jefferson as Secretary of State had to warn Genet to get rid of his privateers and commission no more. The Frenchman promised to comply but secretly armed another, broke a promise to Jefferson, and sent the offender, named *The Little Sarah,* out to sea. The arrogant Genet had hoped to bring America, still officially France's "ally"

John Jay, first Chief Justice, wrote extensively on foreign affairs for The Federalist.

under the Treaty of 1778, into the war on her side, but this was not the way to do it.

Hamilton in the meantime had taken the young British minister, George Hammond, under his wing. Between the pressures of the two diplomats, Washington's patience was severely tried. He was relieved when he learned that at last even Jefferson was worried about Genet's conduct. With support from Jefferson, the cabinet asked France to recall her representative in the summer of 1793. Hamilton was pleased also, but his triumph was not complete. Another French minister now arrived, sent by a new ruling faction in Paris, with orders to have

Genet sent home, presumably to be guillotined. Washington refused and allowed Genet to stay in the United States. Jefferson resigned as Secretary of State and was succeeded early in January, 1794, by Edmund Randolph, but Washington was really leaning on Hamilton for advice on foreign affairs, which only grew more complicated.

Jay's controversial treaty

George Washington was anxious to do more than just stay out of war. He wanted to cultivate friendly commercial relations with European nations, particularly England. Despite the Revolution, England remained America's best customer, and the President knew that to prosper, his country must trade. Accordingly, he sent John Jay to London in the spring of 1794 with instructions to negotiate a commercial treaty.

Jay's was a difficult task. His nation was young and unsettled; it had failed to live up to some of its treaty obligations contracted in 1783, and despite Hamilton's efforts, its credit was not yet stable enough to inspire confidence in foreign financial circles.

Yet Jay was supposed to get the British to evacuate the Northwest military posts, and to make them stop encouraging Indian raids on American settlements in the Northwest Territory. He was instructed to persuade Britain to stop seizing American shipping as part of her attempt to blockade the French, and to cease "impressing" American seamen. (So terrible was the life of ordinary seamen in the royal navy of that era that they would desert and ship on American merchant ships whenever they could. In consequence, British men-of-war would search United States ships for their subjects—or supposed subjects—and "impress" them into service.)

After many months of negotiation, Jay came back with a treaty that caused a storm. He had got the British to agree to leave the military posts by 1796, but matters relating to our northern boundary, the settlement of prewar debts, and compensation for British naval seizures were referred to commissions of arbitration, to be settled at a later date. Commercially, America wrung a few concessions out of the British. But nothing was said about impressment or the Indians menacing our frontiers.

When all this was known on this side of the Atlantic, Jay's reputation sank. He had sold out to the British, America's old enemies, and hurt America's friends, the French. He was hanged in effigy, and Hamilton, defending Jay in public, was stoned by a mob. Southern planters and Northern traders were alike unhappy, and even Washington was displeased, for all thought Jay had conceded too much and won too little. But with Hamilton's support, Washington urged the Senate to ratify the treaty as something better than nothing. By a vote of 20 to 10, the exact number needed, the Senators complied, although many of them had been in disagreement with the treaty.

Not long after, George Washington decided to retire. His supporters had persuaded him to run again in 1792, using the argument that his help was needed in getting the new ship of state safely under way. But now affairs appeared to be in much better condition, and the old general turned to writing his farewell address. With the aid of such friends as Alexander Hamilton and James Madison, he set down his last official advice to his countrymen in the fall of 1796. He warned against the danger of the party system and urged his fellow citizens to observe financial good faith and cultivate peace with all countries, suggesting that the nation's remote geographical situation called for a policy of isolation from European affairs.

President John Adams

With Washington in retirement, the Federalists nominated John Adams, and the Democratic-Republicans, with new hope for the Presidency, ran Jefferson against him. Jefferson came within three electoral votes of winning. President Adams, whom Franklin called always honest, often great, and sometimes mad, tried his best to help the Federalists maintain their grip upon the machinery of government, but that young party was already splitting at the seams. Hamilton and his faction did not trust the New Englander. They were further alarmed at his friendship with Jefferson, who had become Vice-President by virtue of coming in second in the election. Blocked at every turn by the Democratic-Republicans in Congress, sometimes ill-served by his friends, and saddled with a poor cabinet, Adams did not enjoy his stay in the White House.

It was in diplomacy that John Adams scored his biggest triumph. Shortly before he came to office, the Jay treaty was put into effect. Although that document professed not to violate any American treaties with the French, it was nevertheless hostile to that nation in spirit. Because the Federalists, particularly Hamilton, were friendly to the British, it was obvious that the treaty would be interpreted in their favor. But reports from Paris made it clear that there would be trouble over the matter.

In fact, when Adams sent Charles Cotesworth Pinckney as United States minister to France in December, 1796, the French refused to receive him. Then, in May, 1797, Adams appointed a three-man commission—Pinckney, John Marshall, and Elbridge Gerry— to obtain a treaty of commerce and friendship with France. Talleyrand, the French foreign minister, delegated three agents (later referred to by the Americans in their dispatches as X, Y, and Z) to meet Adams' representatives, and these three suggested a United States loan to France, along with a bribe of $240,000, as their conditions for a commercial treaty. The

Americans indignantly refused, and Adams brought the matter before Congress, giving it his commission's correspondence concerning X, Y, and Z. Tempers flared. War seemed imminent. George Washington was asked to come out of retirement to lead the army, and a Navy Department was formally established.

Though neither France nor America made a formal declaration of war, an undeclared naval war was begun in November, 1798, when the French captured the American schooner *Retaliation* off Guadeloupe. A number of naval battles ensued in which both French and American ships were captured or destroyed. The Federalists, avowedly anti-French after the radical excesses of the French Revolution, whipped up anti-French feeling to a hysterical point and then enacted some of the most vindictive and undemocratic legislation this country has ever known, all in the name of national security. In June, 1798, they pushed through Congress the Naturalization and Alien Acts. The former extended the requirements of residence before citizenship from five years to 14, and the latter empowered the President to expel undesirable foreigners.

To seal the doom of their enemies, the Federalists also passed a Sedition Act, providing punishment for anyone opposing the execution of the laws or aiding any "riot" or "unlawful assembly," or even anyone who published "any false, scandalous, and malicious writing" which defamed the

Congress or the President. This law sought to silence the Democratic-Republican editors who were sniping at the administration, and sent some of them to jail. Jefferson's followers were so discouraged that one of them suggested to him the dissolution of the Union. However, the answer lay not in breaking up the Union but in a violent protest from the states. Jefferson, the leading advocate of states' rights, drafted a strong resolution against the abuse of central power by the national government; it was formally endorsed by Kentucky lawmakers in 1798. A similar protest, written by James Madison, was shortly approved by the Virginia legislature. The Kentucky and Virginia resolutions held, in general, that the Union was a compact between the states and that as members they had the right to "interpose" when the central government acted in a way not specifically allowed

The monster is the five-headed Directory that ruled France in 1797 and asked the three American representatives for a bribe in the infamous XYZ affair.

in the Constitution—that is, to declare unlawful such legislation as the Alien and Sedition Acts. Although the Supreme Court later maintained that the expulsion of aliens was the business of the central government, these resolutions caused many people to wonder about the nature of the Union, a question that was not settled until the Civil War, if then.

In 1800, when Napoleon Bonaparte had assumed power, French-American hostilities came to an end with the Treaty of Morfontaine, more usually known as the Convention of 1800. This treaty released the United States from its defensive alliance with France and opened the way for increased commerce between the two nations.

The revolution of 1800

Jefferson had no trouble getting his party's nomination in 1800. The party caucus threw its weight behind him and supported glib Aaron Burr of New York, a popular local politician, for the Vice-Presidency. Burr also gained the backing of the New York legislature, which in turn chose the electors. Hamilton thereupon angrily asked for a special session of the legislature to shake loose Burr's grip, but John Jay, who had resigned from the Supreme Court to accept the governorship of New York, politely turned him down.

When the ballots were counted, Jefferson and Burr, both members of the same party, were tied, with 73 votes each. John Adams, running again, had only 65 votes, and his Federalist running mate, C. C. Pinckney, 64. The strange tie between Jefferson and Burr meant that the decision was now up to the House of Representatives. A Federalist House found itself obliged to elect an opposing President, or at least to choose between two members of the other party. The balloting was carried on past mid-February, 1801, with the Representatives in a deadlock. Then Alexander Hamilton made a decision. Swallowing his dislike of Jefferson, he turned against Aaron Burr, who had so recently snatched the New York ballots from the Federalists, and threw his influence to Jefferson. Hamilton hated but respected Jefferson; he hated and distrusted Burr, who remains up to our time a disputed, unloved figure in history.

With Hamilton's statesmanlike action, which would cost him his life on a dueling ground a few years later, the period of Federalist domination came to a close. The Federalists, a good many of whom feared rule by the mob, now shuddered as they waited for the United States to fall into the hands of a Democratic-Republican executive and legislature. With Jefferson, whom they regarded as a wild radical, in power, anarchy would surely be the order of the day. They were to find their fears vastly exaggerated. When the scholarly Virginian took the helm, he demonstrated an axiom that the decades were to bear out: Liberal candidates often make conservative Presidents.

COLLECTION OF IRVING S. OLDS

THE WAR AT SEA

The American Revolution brought political independence to the United States. It took another war to gain recognition for the young country as an equal partner with Great Britain in world commerce. Following the Revolution, the British tried to place as many restrictions on American shipping on the Atlantic and on the Great Lakes as they had in colonial days. The powerful royal navy enforced these rules, seizing and impounding American vessels and crews that broke them. After many such incidents and numerous diplomatic protests, it became apparent that the small United States Navy would have to defend America's rights as a sovereign nation if she wanted to trade where and with whom she pleased. And so the War of 1812 began as a naval conflict. New ships were built and old ships were refitted, and an eager group of young officers was given commands. In two years of fighting, the United States Navy succeeded in doing what before then had seemed impossible: It wrested control of the American shipping lanes from the powerful hands of the British by fighting the royal navy to a standoff.

THE BIRTH OF A NAVAL POWER

Commodore Isaac Hull (above) commanded the American warship *Constitution* in her famous battle with the British *Guerriere*. The defeat of the *Guerriere* was the first major sea victory of the war.

The frigate *United States* is shown at the left, flying the flags of the world on her launching day in 1797. It was customary for an important naval vessel to begin her career with this kind of display.

OVERLEAF: The masts of the once-proud *Guerriere* splinter and fall under a withering barrage of cannon fire from the *Constitution*. This fierce duel was fought in the choppy waters off the coast of Halifax, Nova Scotia, on August 19, 1812.

THE MACEDONIAN

Captain Stephen Decatur first won fame as an American naval officer in 1804, fighting the Barbary pirates. In 1812, he was the captain of the *United States,* on the prowl for British warships.

Both the *United States* and the *Macedonian* had the same basic design as this powerful square-rigged frigate.

On October 25, 1812, Decatur's *United States* (below, right) sighted the British frigate *Macedonian* (below, left), and in a brilliant series of maneuvers she succeeded in delivering a crippling broadside blast to the enemy ship.

1.

3.

THE WAR AT SEA

THE CONSTITUTION

On December 29, 1812, near Brazil, the *Constitution* struck another blow at British sea power. Here the famous American warship (later known as Old Ironsides) under Commodore Bainbridge defeated the British frigate *Java*. These four aquatints were made from on-the-spot sketches by a Lieutenant Buchanan. The first three trace the destruction of the *Java* under the furious assault of the *Constitution*.

WILLIAM BAINBRIDGE

2.

4.

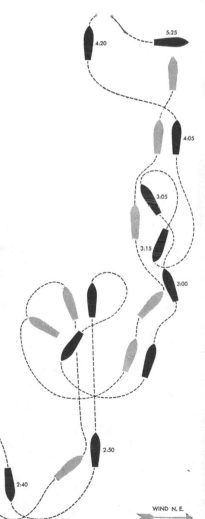

4:20   5:25

4:05

3:05

3:15

3:00

2:50

2:40

TIME—2:10 P. M.

JAVA

CONSTITUTION

WIND N. E.

The diagram at the right records the steps by which the *Constitution* defeated the *Java,* from the first encounter at 2:10 p.m. to the final surrender at 5:25. At the end of the battle the masts of the British ship had been shot away, and she had been leveled almost to the waterline. After the survivors were removed to the *Constitution,* the *Java* was blown up, as shown above in the fourth aquatint.

AN AMERICAN DEFEAT

JAMES LAWRENCE

The war at sea was no unbroken series of American victories. One of the worst setbacks for the United States Navy occurred off Boston on June 1, 1813. The British *Shannon,* cruising just beyond the harbor, challenged the Américan *Chesapeake* to a ship-to-ship duel (left). When the two crashed together, British seamen swarmed off the deck, platforms, and rigging of their ship and onto the *Chesapeake,* where the crews met in open combat. Both sides suffered heavy losses, but the British, fighting savagely and with great experience, were the victors. During the fierce battle aboard the *Chesapeake,* Captain Lawrence (above, left, in white breeches and blue jacket) was mortally wounded. As he lay dying, he gave his final order, which became the rallying cry for the American navy: "Don't give up the ship!"

327

THE WAR AT SEA

ON LAKE ERIE

In 1813, the royal navy controlled the St. Lawrence River and Lake Erie. Supplies for British troops on America's northern borders were brought inland on these waterways. To meet this British menace, a nine-ship fleet was built by the Americans in Erie, Pennsylvania, and placed under the command of a young officer, Oliver Hazard Perry. On September 10, 1813, the American and British fleets met on Lake Erie (above). Perry's flagship, the *Lawrence,* carried a banner with the inspiring last words of Captain Lawrence on it. At a crucial point in the battle, the *Lawrence* was disabled, and Perry calmly took his flag and went aboard the undamaged *Niagara.* In the engraving at the left, of the longboat nearing the new flagship, Perry is standing in the stern of the boat. Victory on Lake Erie came to the Americans after a long, hard battle. When the British had surrendered, Perry sent the now-famous message to Major General Harrison: "We have met the enemy and they are ours."

OLIVER HAZARD PERRY

329

On the night of September 13–14, 1814, a British fleet bombarded American-held Fort McHenry (above, center) just off Chesapeake Bay. British troops were marching on Baltimore, and the fort was one of the few defenses that stood in their way. The little fort repulsed the assault, however, and the British fleet withdrew.

Francis Scott Key was on an American truce ship held by the British until after the bombardment. When he saw his country's flag still flying in the "dawn's early light," he wrote *The Star-Spangled Banner*, which was to become the lyric of our national anthem. Below is his later copy of one of the five verses.

O say can you see, ~~through~~ by the dawn's early light,
What so proudly we hail'd at the twilight's last gleaming,
Whose broad stripes & bright stars through the perilous fight
O'er the ramparts we watch'd, were so gallantly streaming?
And the rocket's red glare, the bomb bursting in air,
Gave proof through the night that our flag was still there,
O say does that star spangled banner yet wave
O'er the land of the free & the home of the brave?

THE STAR-SPANGLED BANNER

SMITHSONIAN INSTITUTION

All that remains of the star-spangled banner that flew over Fort McHenry during the British bombardment is this battered remnant that now hangs in the Smithsonian Institution in Washington, D.C. This second U.S. flag, 1795–1818, had 15 stars and 15 stripes.

CHAPTER 12

THE REPUBLICAN ERA

When Thomas Jefferson and his party, the Democratic-Republican, replaced the Federalists in 1801, conservative people expected all kinds of trouble, even revolution. But his inaugural address should have somewhat allayed their fears. Trying to smooth out the party bitterness that had erupted while Adams was in office, he said, "We are all Republicans! We are all Federalists!" He wanted the central government to enjoy its full constitutional powers, but he hoped there would be as little federal regulation as possible. Conservatives were relieved to hear him affirm the rights of individual states and to recommend that national expenditures be reduced.

As the new President looked around him, he must have concluded that he needed to move slowly. Washington itself typified the country at large: It was new and primitive, a morass of mud dotted with boardinghouses and shanties. It was inhabited by about 3,000 people, 600 of whom were

Oliver Hazard Perry is shown on his flagship Lawrence *before a banner bearing the words, "Don't give up the ship."*

slaves. The new Capitol was still unfinished, and so was the President's house. Its roof leaked, the walls were not all plastered, and the floor had already begun to sag as the green lumber shrank. A United States map showed that three new states had joined the 13 original colonies—Vermont, Kentucky, and Tennessee.

On the day before Jefferson took office, the hated sedition laws expired. He had thought them unconstitutional and quickly pardoned those few men still in jail under their provisions. His administration also repealed the liquor taxes that had brought on the Whiskey Rebellion; they had cost as much to enforce as they collected in revenue. Jefferson made another popular move when he appointed Albert Gallatin as Secretary of the Treasury. The Swiss-born financier, a former teacher of French at Harvard College, lived up to the tradition of Alexander Hamilton in many respects. He was a genius with figures; he was determined to balance the budget. And the new Democratic-Republican regime seemed bent upon keeping its promises of economy. Old sailors paled when they learned what was in store

The Capitol around 1800, during the Presidency of John Adams, was only partially completed. It was without the wings and the modern dome it has today.

for them, for Jefferson viewed the naval force as a defensive instrument. He liked the idea already suggested by John Adams that the deep-water navy be reduced in favor of small gunboats suitable for coastal defense.

Yet in spite of Jefferson's determination to avoid a large navy, the United States became involved in a naval war soon after he took office. In a sense, the Tripolitan War was a legacy from the two previous administrations. Both Washington and Adams had continued the practice, begun by the British, of paying tribute to the Barbary States of Algiers, Morocco, Tripoli, and Tunis in order to insure noninterference with American commerce along the North Afri-

can coast. In May, 1801, the pasha of Tripoli increased his demands for tribute, and when Jefferson hesitated, he declared war on the United States. Commodore Edward Preble was named to lead the American naval forces in the Mediterranean. Although fighting 4,000 miles away from home, and with only the most meager financial support from Congress, the young navy distinguished itself. In June, 1805, a peace treaty favorable to United States interests was signed with Tripoli.

Napoleon makes a sale

To Jefferson, and to the United States, there now came a sudden piece of good fortune. Ever since the Treaty of Paris in 1783, when the western American boundary was set at the Mississippi River, the government had nervously watched as the Spanish occasionally interfered with frontiersmen living in the great valley. In 1762, when French power in North America was breaking up in the last of the French and Indian Wars, Spain had obtained all the vast areas at the foot of the river—and to the west—by the Treaty of Fontainebleau. It was called Louisiana, after the great Louis XIV, but it included much more than Louisiana today. It was an ill-defined area stretching west from the Mississippi, altogether vague in its frontiers.

Then, in 1800, a surprising thing happened. Napoleon Bonaparte, seizing power after France's brief, disastrous experiment with popular government, put pressure on Charles IV of Spain, and that weak monarch traded Spanish Louisiana for a few small thrones and titles in Italy. This trade, made secretly at the Treaty of San Ildefonso, meant that France, at the height of her power, had replaced Great Britain and Spain as the threat to the American West.

Late in 1802, just before the Spanish handed over Louisiana to France, the Spanish closed New Orleans to American trade, and Americans mistakenly assumed that the French were behind the move. The loss of this major port was disastrous for Western farmers and traders in those prerailroad days, when everything went down the Mississippi. Angry

Albert Gallatin served as Secretary of the Treasury under Jefferson and Madison.

Kentuckians reached for their rifles, ready to fight the French or anyone else who interfered with their trade. Jefferson wrote at once to Robert Livingston, the American minister to France, with instructions to negotiate to have the port reopened. Then he dispatched James Monroe to help, authorizing him to make an offer for New Orleans and West Florida at $2,000,000, and if need be, to go to $10,000,000.

Events worked for America. Napoleon, vexed because the Spanish had been agonizingly slow about turning over Louisiana to him and smarting under a military defeat sustained while trying to suppress black revolt in Haiti, decided to give up his

335

Robert Livingston, Jefferson's minister to France, negotiated the Louisiana Purchase.

new acquisition. It might, he thought, be taken from him at any time by England, with her sea power and bases in North America. Consequently, to the stunned amazement of Livingston and Monroe, he offered to sell them not just New Orleans but all of the boundless Louisiana Territory. Exceeding their authorization, the two representatives agreed to pay approximately $15,000,000—the price of a few highway cloverleaves today—for a vast and beautiful land that doubled the size of the United States.

The treaty of cession was signed in May, 1803, and approved by the Senate that October. The French flag had barely risen again in New Orleans, to the brief joy of the natives, before

it came down, and on December 20, 1803, the Stars and Stripes went up on the old Cabildo, where the Spanish and French councils had sat.

While all this was taking place, Jefferson was already looking to increase our knowledge of the great West—its geography, its peoples, and its resources. Before the purchase was final, he had organized a first transcontinental journey of exploration, headed by Captains Meriwether Lewis and William Clark, brother of the famous George Rogers Clark. On May 14, 1804, they started up the Missouri River on the remarkable trip that would reach the Pacific Ocean in 1805 and bring them safely home a year later.

It was, all in all, one of the greatest bargains in history, better even than the $24 paid for Manhattan by the Dutch—for, payment or not, Europeans would have taken New York, and the same cannot be definitely said of Americans and the West. But the Louisiana Purchase raised thorny questions nevertheless. What of our great principle about the "consent of the governed"? Who had asked the consent of the *habitants* of New Orleans or of the Indian tribes? What about the Constitution and "strict construction"—the principle that the federal government could do nothing not expressly provided by the Constitution? Jefferson searched the sacred document, found little, and became for the moment a "loose constructionist." One must assume, ran

THE LOUISIANA PURCHASE

Doubled the size of the United States
with the addition of
828,000 square miles of territory.

his argument, that a nation can acquire property, and from that must flow the right to govern it.

Although the President's views prevailed, the Federalists also changed their grounds and bitterly contested Jefferson's actions. Behind the legal talk lay their real fear that agrarian and Western interests in the government would gain from the new lands, and that New England and the trading, commercial Northeast would be overshadowed. New England began to fear a great slave empire spreading into the new territory and dominated by Southerners. Curiously, the Yankees were now talking about the importance of strict construction of the Constitution and states' rights. There

was even some discussion of breaking up the Union and establishing a Northern confederacy.

At this time Aaron Burr, the Vice-President, was running for governor in New York, and New England separatists believed he would join in such a secession, once in office. Alexander Hamilton, who thoroughly disliked Burr, was reported as saying that he was "a dangerous man," too untrustworthy to hold office. Hamilton certainly contributed to his enemy's defeat, and this was too much for Burr, who already had suffered from Hamilton's interference in the contested election of 1800. The Vice-President demanded satisfaction. On the west bank of the Hudson, at Weehawken, New Jersey, one July dawn in 1804, Hamilton, the man who, next to Washington, made the new nation a going concern, took a fatal ball directly through the heart. He had avoided shooting Burr. But the career of Burr, who later became involved in a mysterious, possibly treasonable military adventure in the Southwest, was quite finished.

Virginia dynasty

From the beginning, it seemed that the age of Jefferson would be one of peace and progress. With his architects and engineers he made ambitious plans for the capital city. He promoted immigration, and settlement in the West. Ohio entered the Union in 1803. The Louisiana Purchase elated the President, who began to dream of a great voluntary association of free governments covering the whole Western Hemisphere. His Secretary of the Treasury proclaimed a surplus. His popularity was great.

By Jefferson's second election, in 1804, the system of nominating and electing the President and the Vice-President had been changed; the country did not want another tie like that four years before between two men of the same party. This time, Presidential and Vice-Presidential candidates ran together, as a ticket—in the same way they do today—and the Vice-President was no longer just the candidate with the second highest number of votes. With Burr disgraced, Jefferson had George Clinton of New York

with him on the Democratic-Republican ticket. The failure of the Northern confederacy to break up the Union so weakened the Federalists, who put up C. C. Pinckney and Rufus King, that the Jeffersonians carried every state but Connecticut. It was a smashing victory; the Federalist Party never really recovered. It took another drubbing with the same candidates when, in 1808, Jefferson stepped down —following Washington's precedent of two terms—but ran his hand-picked candidate and fellow-Virginian James Madison, again with George Clinton for Vice-President. Madison swept into office to carry on what was becoming known as the Virginia dynasty.

Sparks from Europe

By then, however, there was only one great issue before America—an issue wished upon it from Europe, for in 1803 the Napoleonic Wars broke out again. The mastery of Europe, and the fate of many ancient states and kingdoms, was at stake. The fact that Napoleon at the outset seemed to be the inheritor and champion of "liberty, equality, and fraternity," the slogan of the French Revolution, blinded many in America to the fact that he was a dictator and cruel tyrant. Anti-British feeling in America harked back to the Revolution and the follies of Lord North's ministry and ignored the fact that England from 1784 until North died in 1806 had (with a brief interruption) been governed by William Pitt, the

Younger, a greater enemy of tyranny than Americans themselves.

Fortunately for free government—in the long view of history—the British also had a fleet. If the Battle of Austerlitz in 1805 gave Bonaparte control of the land, the victory at Trafalgar, although it cost the life of Lord Nelson, gave Britain the seas. In a long struggle lasting until 1815, and at frightful sacrifices to themselves, the British eventually brought Napoleon down. But meanwhile the life of neutrals was difficult; in a death struggle, no one cares much about the rights of bystanders—especially when they are trying to trade with both sides. This, in capsule, is the story of America's relations with Europe between 1804 and 1812, and they culminated in a bloody, unnecessary—yet at moments glorious—final war with England.

In wartime, international law is an early casualty, and American ships suffered abuses at the hands of the belligerents. In only a few years, up through 1807, about 1,500 merchantmen were seized by England and France. The British accused the United States of fraudulent use of its neutral flag, and their attitude became noticeably more hostile. In retaliation, Jefferson, in April, 1806, signed the Non-Importation Act, prohibiting the shipping in of certain goods from England. He vainly hoped the action would cause the British to relax their pressure.

During the same year, Napoleon

About 1800, American sailors were in constant danger of being impressed to serve on British ships. This wood figure representing a sailor of that era was carved as an advertisement to stand before a cigar store.

struck at England with the Berlin Decree, pronouncing all of England under a blockade. The British lashed back in 1807 with the first Order in Council, blockading the entire coast of France. All neutral shipping was warned away from the Continent. Napoleon's answer was the Milan Decree of December, 1807, threatening to confiscate any ship that had entered a British port, paid a tax, or been visited by British officers.

But the grievance that would eventually provoke war was the impressment of American seamen. Thousands were taken off United States ships by the royal navy, and anger was already high when there came what diplomats call an incident.

The Leopard strikes

In February, 1807, four British sailors were known to have jumped ship at Norfolk, Virginia; then they had signed on the American frigate *Chesapeake*. Admiral George C. Berkeley, senior British officer on the North American station, ordered his captains to be on the lookout for them. Late in June, the *Chesapeake* headed for the Mediterranean and, before it was more than a few miles off the Virginia Capes, was hailed by H. M. S. *Leopard*. The American ship's decks were still in confusion and her guns were not ready, but the captain was not concerned. He believed that the British ship merely wanted some dispatches delivered to Europe, a common practice in those days. Upon learning that a search was intended, the American ship refused to heave to and was promptly blasted by three broadsides, which killed three men and wounded 18 others. One of the officers of the *Chesapeake* rushed to the galley for a hot coal and with it touched off one of the guns, but to no avail. The *Chesapeake* hove to. Four men were removed from her crew, but only one of them proved to be a British subject; he was later hanged from the yardarm of his own vessel as a deserter. When the *Chesapeake* limped back into port, tattered and torn, the

In 1811, at Tippecanoe Creek, William Henry Harrison defeated the Indian confederacy and earned his famous nickname.

people went wild with anger. British officers ashore were nearly mobbed, and the Virginia militia had to be called out to preserve order. To Jefferson's credit, there was no war. He could have had it for a whisper, but he chose otherwise.

The embargo

Rather than war, Jefferson chose diplomacy, and into the American language came a word that soon drove New Englanders frantic at its sound. The Embargo Act, called the Dambargo by shippers, was designed to bring the European belligerents to their senses by cutting off American supplies. Passed by Congress in De-

Tenskwatawa, Tecumseh's one-eyed brother, who was also called The Prophet, was defeated by Harrison at Tippecanoe Creek.

cember, 1807, it provided that no goods would leave our ports for Europe. This was like trying to stop a nosebleed by cutting off the patient's head. Ships rotted at the wharves and commercial life came to a standstill. In the absence of foreign goods, domestic manufactures began to grow. But before long, Americans reverted to breaking a law they did not like, just as they had in colonial days, and a thriving smugglers' trade sprang up between the United States and Canada by way of Lake Champlain and other routes. Across the Atlantic there did come complaints from the British, and signs of unrest that made Jefferson vainly hopeful. But then there

were good crops abroad and eventually, just before he handed the government over to James Madison, Jefferson had to suffer the humiliation of the repeal of the Embargo Act as a failure. Meanwhile, it had so angered New England as to start talk of nullifying what Yankee shippers regarded as a pro-French, anti-British law. In the election of 1808, New England went Federalist.

The Madison administration

Madison was known as Little Jemmy, and indeed he was smaller and, to many, less interesting than his popular, gay, and beautifully dressed wife. But when he became President in March, 1809, he was just as intent upon the preservation of peace as Jefferson. The embargo had just been replaced by the Non-Intercourse Act, under which Americans could trade with anyone but the French or British. If either of them stopped violating our neutral rights, of course, trade would be resumed. At this juncture there appeared on the scene David Erskine, the British minister to Washington, who with his American wife was making a most favorable impression in the capital. Erskine said that the hated Orders in Council of 1807, the basis of most of the contention, would be revoked in June of that

OVERLEAF: *Jefferson, his Embargo Act, and its ill effects are lampooned in this English drawing. Napoleon, hiding behind the chair, is prompting Jefferson.*

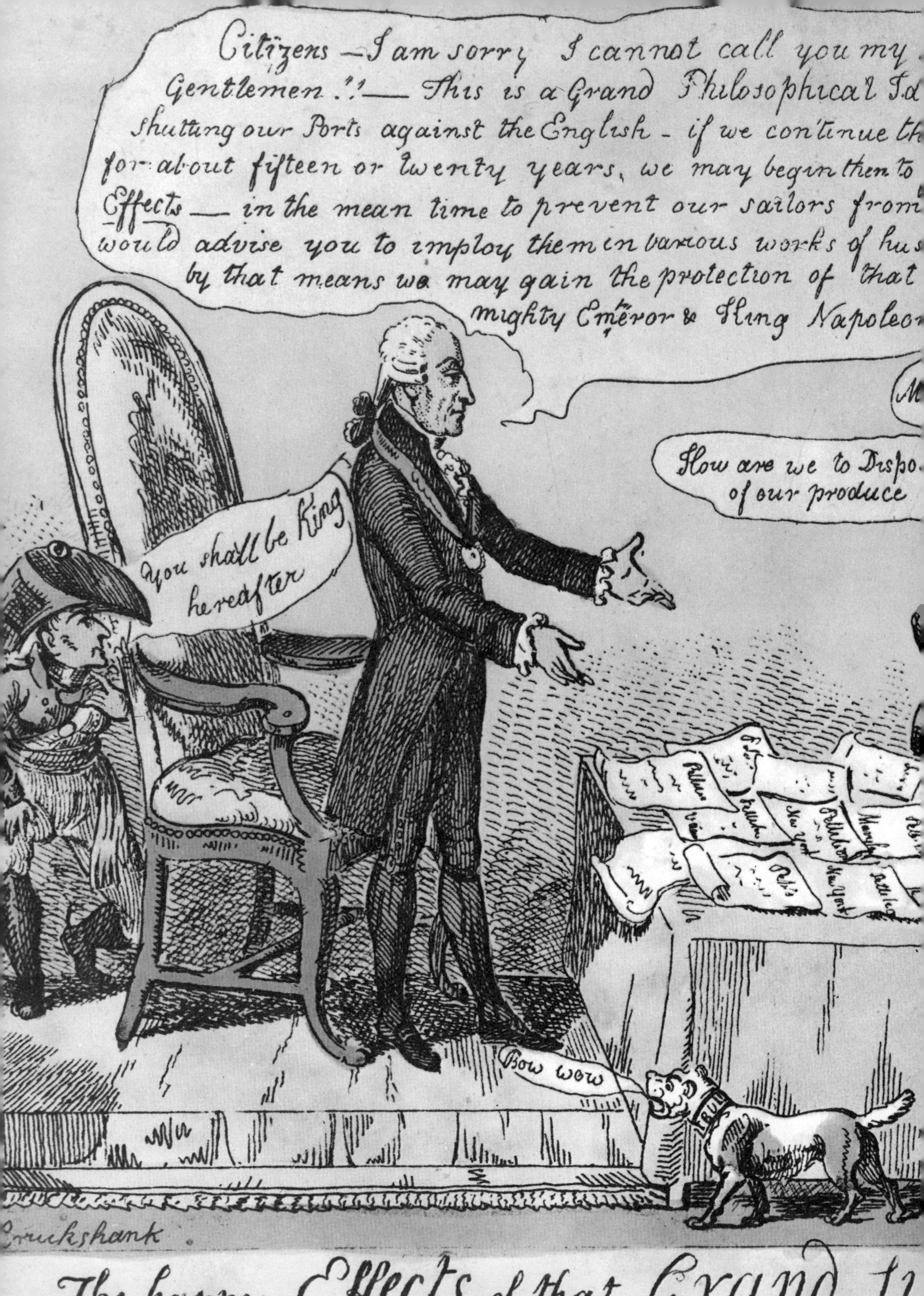

The happy Effects of that Grand Sy

year. Madison, a greenhorn at diplomacy, assumed that the minister had authority for his promise, and legalized trade with Great Britain. Shortly ships were streaming out of American ports bound for England, but Madison was soon disabused of his belief when the British foreign secretary, George Canning, disavowed Erskine's statement. In August, 1809, the President was obliged to reinstate the Non-Intercourse Act against Britain.

Relations with England continued to deteriorate, and the expiration of the Non-Intercourse Act on May 1, 1810, brought no relief. Congress at once supplanted it with a strange piece of legislation called (after its father, Representative Nathaniel Macon of North Carolina) Macon's Bill No. 2. This reopened trade with England and France, but provided that if within a year either country stopped interfering with American shipping, the United States would stop trading with the other one within three months. If neither country acted within the year, non-intercourse would be resumed.

It was the wily Napoleon's turn to fool Madison, and he did so by leading him to believe, quite falsely, that he had cancelled his Berlin and Milan Decrees. Trusting Napoleon's representatives, the President snapped at the bait, warning England in November, 1810, that she would receive no more American goods unless she at once dropped her Orders in Council, too. The British refused for over a year because they knew that Napoleon

had not really complied with Madison's demands, and was still seizing our ships, and that in that era of slow communications, we would not find out for many months. On March 2, 1811, Congress cancelled trade with Great Britain.

The war hawks

Tensions were renewed by news from the frontier. Westerners had long complained that the British were paying the Indians for American scalps, and to punish them, General William Henry Harrison, governor of Indiana Territory, moved against the Ohio tribes, which had been organized into a powerful confederacy by the great Shawnee chief, Tecumseh. The meeting took place at the main Indian town at Tippecanoe Creek in November, 1811, when Tecumseh was absent; it gave Harrison both a victory and a nickname that stuck. As the Indians retreated, British arms were found on the field of battle, and the news was quickly transmitted to members of the newly elected Congress of 1811. Many of the new Congressmen came from the West and South, and their reaction was violent. The "buckskin statesmen"—or the war hawks, as John Randolph of Roanoke, the brilliant Virginia eccentric, called these members—were ready to fight. Young Henry Clay of Kentucky, one of the loudest voices, became Speaker of the House, and the Congressional halls now resounded with talk of war.

The war party had its way. "I prefer

the troubled ocean of war . . . with all its calamities . . . to the tranquil and putrescent pool of ignominious peace!" cried Clay.

"Mr. Madison's war"

By June 1, 1812, Madison, who still refused to believe the British when they said Napoleon had deceived him, was driven to declare war. His message recommending it was approved at once by the House, 79 to 49, and after a few days of argument, by the more reluctant Senate, 19 to 13. On June 18, Madison signed the declaration. Thoroughly unprepared for it, the American people were again plunged into conflict with their old adversary. "The blood of the American freemen must flow to cement his [Napoleon's] power," cried the high, angry voice of Randolph.

The War of 1812 is usually regarded as the most unnecessary and unsatisfactory one that America ever fought. It was entered into while news was being brought across the Atlantic that the despised Orders in Council would be suspended. It was bitterly resented by Britons, who felt the United States had stabbed them in the back while they were holding off a menace to civilization. And it concluded with the bloody, pointless Battle of New Orleans, fought two weeks after the peace treaty was signed.

As the military campaigns opened, the Americans carried out their threats and lunged at Canada, but were defeated in each attempt. General William Hull led raw American militia across the border, by way of Detroit, in July, 1812, but soon timidly withdrew. At once Isaac Brock, an excellent British general, rushed troops to Detroit from Niagara. When Brock suggested to Hull that unless he surrendered promptly, the Indian allies

The American attempt to take Canada in 1812 failed because the New York militia refused to support the regulars (in red) who had a toehold at Queenston.

On August 15, 1814, under the command of General Edmund Gaines, 2,000 Americans at Fort Erie repulsed the English attack led by General Gordon Drummond.

of the redcoats might get out of hand in the assault, the dithering defender of the city promptly surrendered without firing a shot. At Fort Dearborn, the present site of Chicago, the garrison evacuated, only to be massacred —men, women, and children—by Potawatomi Indians. Tecumseh threw in his lot with the English. At a single stroke, the American line of defense was thrown back to the Wabash and Ohio Rivers.

An American attempt to take Niagara also failed when the New York militia declined to support the regulars in the battle, causing another withdrawal. Madison's incompetent General Henry Dearborn then tried

an assault against Montreal in November, by way of Lake Champlain, but after marching a few miles, his men balked at crossing the border, on the ground that they had not signed up to fight beyond it. The general turned his troops around and marched back to camp.

The Great Lakes, if they provided a strong barrier against the enemy's land forces, also posed a grave threat from local British fleets. Before the year 1812 was out, it became clear that America must have both a freshwater and a salt-water navy. During the winter of 1812–13, Captain Oliver Hazard Perry directed the construction from green local timbers of an

American flotilla on Lake Erie. By the summer of 1813, he was on the prowl, searching for enemy craft. He found his prey in the early days of September, at Put-in-Bay, north of the mouth of the Sandusky River in Ohio, and in a bloody three-hour fight won a decisive victory.

Having obtained control of Lake Erie, American troops under General "Tippecanoe" Harrison were able in 1813 to invade Canada, where, at the Battle of the Thames, Chief Tecumseh was slain. This disheartened the Indians and helped secure the Northwest. Other campaigns entered Canada at several points, and in one the capital of Upper Canada, York (now Toronto), was seized and its public buildings burned, a deed that the British remembered when they took Washington. But no real results came of all this fighting. Two attempts to take Montreal fizzled out, and the invasion of Canada was a dismal failure.

Meanwhile, the British had raided and blockaded the coasts until great distress was felt throughout the country. Madison was re-elected with a much-reduced margin over an antiwar party heavily supported by disaffected New England, where active trading with the enemy was going on. The only good news came now and then from the heady exploits of the tiny salt-water navy. At the outset of the war, America had but three major warships, and it was their task to fight off what the British navy could spare from fighting Napoleon. A few days after Hull's surrender at Detroit, his young nephew, Captain Isaac Hull, commanding the *Constitution,* met the *Guerriere* and battered her to bits. In October, the *Wasp* defeated the British vessel *Frolic,* and a week later the *United States* captured the *Macedonian,* taking her to New London as a prize of war.

Disaster in Washington

European events changed the complexion of the war in 1814. The allies entered Paris, forced Napoleon to abdicate, and thus freed thousands of British soldiers for use in Canada. By August, more than 10,000 of the Duke of Wellington's crack troops were assembled at Montreal, ready to crush the Americans once and for all in a mighty counteroffensive.

Commanding General Sir George Prevost now moved southward along Lake Champlain. But after a British naval defeat there, he retreated to Canada. To support that badly managed campaign, other British forces landed at Chesapeake Bay and marched on Washington. About 95,-000 American militiamen were summoned to defend their capital, but only 7,000 appeared, commanded by an incompetent general, William Winder, who soon fled from the British regulars, a much smaller force. British officers that evening sat down to a meal prepared for President and Mrs. Madison, who had fled with little but a few papers, some silver, a Stuart portrait of Washington, and

Dolley's parrot. As the Britons dined, their troops burned public buildings throughout the city in retaliation for York.

The invaders now moved on to besiege Baltimore and bombarded Fort McHenry, during which action Francis Scott Key was inspired to produce the words to *The Star-Spangled Banner*. Just before, the British General Robert Ross, who had dined so well at the White House, was mortally wounded as his forces attempted another landing, and the Chesapeake campaign was called off.

In November, 1814, the British undertook still another thrust. From their base at Jamaica, 7,500 veterans of the Napoleonic campaigns set out through the Gulf of Mexico for an assault on New Orleans. Early in January, General Edward Pakenham sent his British regulars against the 4,500 Americans who defended the city under the bold, brawling General Andrew Jackson, already the winner in a frontier war against the Creek Indians of Alabama. From behind cotton bales piled up as breastworks, the Westerners issued a withering, accurate rifle fire that killed hundreds of enemy soldiers, attacking in close ranks, with flags flying and drums beating the deathly step. No thought of flanking or choosing a better field seems to have assailed the British general's rigid mind. It was Bunker Hill all over again, as if British generals would never learn. Pakenham fell dead; the second in command took over and was promptly struck down; his replacement also died before the blazing Kentucky long rifles. More than 2,000 disciplined redcoats were killed or wounded in two suicidal attacks before the surviving British withdrew and re-embarked. American losses were 13 killed and 58 wounded. The fact that the battle was fought after peace terms were agreed upon did not lessen the gratification of Americans. They could say they had at last won a great battle, and that did much for national pride, even if no one had won a war. Andrew Jackson, of course, had won a great deal, although this affliction to quiet and conservative people still lay far in the future.

American diplomats had sought peace almost from the outset of the war. On June 12, 1812, a week after entering it but before signing the declaration, Madison asked Secretary of State James Monroe to begin peace negotiations. All he wanted was to have the British give up impressment. During the war, the administration clung to the demand, gradually weakening its stand as the military situation worsened. By June, 1814, American peace commissioners were given permission to stop mentioning it altogether. During that summer, the British suggested a conference at the Belgian town of Ghent, and five American representatives turned up in August to hear their proposals.

The most important aspect of the Peace of Ghent is that it meant a ces-

A view of the Battle of New Orleans from behind the British lines shows the British General Pakenham dying in the arms of an aide after being hit three times.

sation of hostilities. Nothing was said about neutral rights, or blockade, or impressment. Most of the day's burning questions were set aside, to be settled later by commissions. No boundaries were changed; no war reparations were assessed; no privileges were surrendered. All prisoners were returned. Neither side won anything tangible in the nearly three years of fighting. America had lost 1,877 men in action. This was fewer, to be sure, than the number who perished in many single ships in World Wars I and II—but that only reflects the rising horror of scientific war, not the importance of the struggle in which the men of 1812 gave their lives.

Although the War of 1812 might be called a second war for independence, at the end of it America was still economically dependent on Britain. But the war did bring to an end an era in American politics. It was the Federalists in New England who had opposed it, most bitterly in the winter of 1814, at the Hartford Convention, when there had been long and strong talk of secession and a separate peace. But Jackson's victory at New Orleans a year later virtually destroyed the Federalist Party, for it became identified with something close to treason. The Democratic-Republicans, though split into occasional factions, were left as the only party of importance, and for a while partisan feeling subsided.

Americans came out of the war with mixed feelings. During it, they had been hopelessly divided. Now there was a tendency to forget the dissension and look again to the task of building a nation. Putting their international troubles behind them, they faced westward and plunged into domestic affairs, united more than ever before by a struggle that was in most respects a failure.

MAIN TEXT CONTINUES IN VOLUME 5

Charles Willson Peale painted this portrait of himself in the long room of the museum he operated on the second floor of Independence Hall from 1802–26. To the right is the mastodon he dug up, and to the left, above the stuffed birds, portraits of Revolutionary heroes.

The Many-Faceted Mr. Peale

A SPECIAL CONTRIBUTION BY
OLIVER JENSEN

A portrait painter, the founder of a great museum, a scientist and inventor, Charles Willson Peale embodied the spirit of American individualism.

The aide-de-camp strode into the painting room and handed a message to General Washington, who was sitting for his portrait, a miniature for Mrs. Washington. "Ah," he remarked after a mere glance, "Burgoyne is defeated." And then, supremely honoring his young friend the artist, that imperturbable man put aside the dispatch for later study and resumed the pose.

Like Burgoyne, Washington was in good hands. The painter, Charles Willson Peale, a slender Marylander with a long nose and a gentle, curious expression, was well known to him. Peale had taken his likeness at Mount Vernon in 1772, as a colonel of Virginia militia, and again in July, 1776. He had been his fellow campaigner only recently at Trenton, Princeton, and Germantown, a dutiful if not a martial figure who carried both a musket and a palette and who, Washington had noted approvingly while riding by one day, was not above gathering the volunteer company he commanded in a field and cooking them a hot meal. Before his public career was over, Washington was to be painted seven times from life by Peale, more times than by any other artist. It was not always an easy job, as the general noted himself. "At first," he wrote Francis Hopkinson in 1785, "I was as impa-

tient . . . and as restive under the operation as a colt is of the saddle. The next time I submitted very reluctantly, but with less flouncing. Now no dray moves more readily to the thill, than I to the painter's chair."

Peale was much more than the faithful painter of Washington; he was one of the universal men of the 18th century, a man whose talent and interests ran in a hundred different directions—inventor, mechanic, silversmith, watchmaker, millwright, patriot, soldier, politician, and naturalist. His hands could make anything his brain devised, from moving pictures to a new type of bridge. He practiced every branch of the graphic arts—oils, water colors, etching, mezzotint—and he was also a sculptor. He painted most of the heroes of the Revolution from life. He was on friendly, sometimes intimate terms with most of the great figures of his age, with men like Franklin, Lafayette, Benjamin West, Jefferson, Madison, and Thomas Paine. If he had done nothing else, he would deserve to be remembered for founding America's first public art gallery and its first museum of natural history. Although he lived most of his life a few hurried paces ahead of the sheriff, he reared one of the world's happiest and most accomplished families. Under his instruction, dozens of his children and relatives learned to wield the brush. Painting was the cottage industry, and the Peales produced more artists than the Adams family did statesmen, or the Beechers preachers.

Peale himself, however, had no high opinion of his own work at the easel, taking the ac-

351

cepted contemporary view that "history" was the proper ambition of the painter. To paint great canvases filled with inspiration and allegory and crowded with generals in dress uniform and 18th-century statesmen in togas, in the manner of Benjamin West and John Trumbull, raised the humble "limner" to the heights of art, and in this field he doubted his ability.

Modest in some ways, Peale also loved to shine, sending notices to the papers every time he launched a fresh project. Nevertheless, he was in every way a likable friend, always bustling and enthusiastic, terrified by the prospect of inactivity, a man who reminds us of Franklin, who respected him, and Jefferson, who so loved and admired him that he sent his grandson to live with the Peales, for his instruction.

In his ideas, Peale was a disciple of the bubbling Age of Reason, a nominal Anglican who was really a Deist, a soldier with a heart so full of affection for all creatures that he became eventually a complete pacifist, a fiery revolutionary so eager to keep on friendly terms with his conservative opponents that he at length forswore politics because of the hard feelings they engendered. Having unwittingly helped

This large portrait of his family was painted by Peale in 1773. Holding a palette and standing in front of an easel, he bends over and watches his brother St. George sketch their mother (far right). His wife Rachel is seated (center), and his brother James smiles at St. George.

expound the unity of science, art, and morality, and the glory of God and Nature.

Peale's own family was not the least extraordinary of his creations, and amused his own contemporaries, especially when he dug into a dictionary of names of classic painters and gave his sons names like Raphaelle, Rembrandt, Rubens, Titian, and Vandyke, artists whose work he knew only by reputation. Female artists were even harder to unearth, and on two of his little girls he inflicted the jawbreaking names of Angelica Kaufmann and Sophonisba Angusciola. When his attention shifted to science from art, he named two more boys Linnaeus and Franklin, until the second of his three wives put her foot down and demanded a plain Elizabeth.

Altogether, over 40 years, the virile Charles Willson Peale sired 17 children, not counting an 18th who was lost in the childbed death of his second wife. The household included not only his own children but those of his brother and sister, together with various transients—black, white, and American Indian. He took in, as an art student, the orphan (and deaf mute) son of General Hugh Mercer; he helped a struggling 17-year-old artist with mechanical ideas, named Robert Fulton. There were also brothers and sisters and other relatives, not to mention live bears, birds, and snakes, an elk, and a five-legged cow with two tails—a gift to the museum that provided apparently normal dairy products for the household.

It was a house full of paints and brushes, the clanking of homemade machinery driving away flies, and of music, for nearly everyone sang and played some instrument. Peale could manufacture a fiddle or a xylophone or whatever was required. The place reeked of chemical experiment. Fumes of arsenic, used as a preservative in taxidermy, rose from the kitchen; gunpowder was also manufactured in it; there was a patent "improved fireplace," a

rouse the wartime mob in Philadelphia, he would place himself before the object of its wrath and strive to send the rioters home, and provide carriages for fleeing Tory ladies, and try to save the property, and the feelings, of the other side.

Everything that Peale undertook began in a burst of optimism. Whether it was his apple-paring machine or his polygraph (a device for duplicating letters), his portable steam bath or his new museum, he was certain that it would revolutionize some aspect of life and perpetual oven, and a great deal of work afoot in leather, glass, and porcelain, inasmuch as the head of the family not only made shoes and eyeglasses but also, to the embarrassment of his more socially ambitious children, liked to manufacture false teeth, of a rather modern design, for himself and his friends, and thought seriously in his later years of turning dentist.

This jack-of-all-trades cherished throughout life a number of unorthodox ideas, some of them since justified in the course of history. His medical opinions, for example, were progressive, and, if for no other reason than that he kept most of the bloodletting doctors of the day away from his house, they seemed effective. He ate sparingly, avoided liquor and tobacco (although he made wine on his farm and could not cure his third wife of dipping snuff), and set great store by exercise, proper posture, and a few bowel purgatives that he liked to press on friends. To all his children he was an indulgent, impartial father, modern in his ideas, adamant against the rod, eager to share in their games, striving to interest them in drawing, nature, and what he called "the mechanic arts." He entertained a high opinion, for the times, of the capabilities of women, and saw no reason why his daughters and nieces should not ride the velocipede he devised or why they should not become painters. In the end, several of them succeeded as artists, and one, Sarah Miriam Peale, hung out her shingle as the first American woman painter with a full-scale professional career.

Some of his notions, however, have still not won any general acceptance. He believed that the normal span of a man's life, provided he lived properly and wore loose-fitting garments, should be 200 years (based on the theory that the natural period of maturity in animals is 10 times the length of the immature period). He later revised the figure downward to 112 and seemed, as he reached 86, full of skill and power, well on the road to achieving it. Sharing with the fieriest Whigs a deep faith in the natural rights and equality of all men, he carried the reasoning a step further to the conclusion that there was no such thing as "inborn" talent. Any intelligent man who applied himself, he announced, could learn to be an artist, for example, and, as if to prove his point, set out to teach all his children and nearly all his other relatives the art of painting.

Outrageous and improbable as these theories are, Peale nearly succeeded in proving both of them. He was never so fit, so eupeptic, or so skilled with the brush as in his 70s and 80s. That Peale, who was born in 1741, did not live until 1941 (or at least to 1853, on the revised estimate) indicates, as the old man would probably contend, no fault in the theory, but simply foolishness on his part. He was the first to acknowledge his own shortcomings, to apologize for false accusations, taking newspaper advertisements to make sure his amends reached everyone. In this case, Peale would have admitted, he died because he overstrained his heart, carrying out a feat that would have killed most men half his age. In the middle of the winter of 1827, cold and exhausted, he carried a trunk on his back for a whole mile along a wood path just to save a little time. He was 86, and out courting a prospective fourth wife. Even then, he survived for several months. Death found the old experimenter studying his own failing pulse.

As for the other theory, it is a matter of record that because of Peale's determination, most of the family he instructed in art became good amateurs and at least six of them skilled professionals—among them Rembrandt, Rubens, and Raphaelle. And this was not the end of the talents the elder Peale stirred to life, for there was his placid, devoted younger brother James, who lived with him for years and, from a helper, graduated into a fine artist in his own right, particularly noted for his miniatures. And there were James' son, a fine water colorist, and his three painting daughters—especially Anna Claypoole Peale, who traveled the country with her father and uncle as a miniaturist.

But there was one thing Charles Willson Peale did not know about his heritage: Artistic talent *did* run in the family. His English-born father, Charles Peale, was gifted with the pen; his forte, forgery. He was caught at last with considerable sums embezzled in

Peale's painting of two of his sons was so realistic that Washington politely nodded to it as he passed.

the course of his job at the General Post Office in London, sentenced to hang and then pardoned on condition he emigrate to America. None of this was ever known to the Peales, and the facts were unearthed only in modern times by Peale's zealous biographer and descendant, Charles Coleman Sellers.

In the new country, Peale, Sr., seems to have conducted himself in an exemplary fashion. A gentleman by birth, educated for a time at Cambridge, he taught school among the plantations of Virginia and Maryland, and died when Charles Willson Peale, his eldest son, was nine, leaving his family in poverty. His widow took to needlework for the rich of Annapolis, and reluctantly apprenticed her son to a saddler when he was 13 years old. The boy applied himself and, prospering, bought a cheap watch. It broke and he learned to fix it. He bought a horse and rode into the coun-

try near Annapolis, where he met, at 18, a girl who attracted him—15-year-old Rachel Brewer—and, with no honeyed words or preparation of any sort, blurted out a proposal, allowing her one hour to make up her mind. (Throughout life, he never changed this head-on method of courtship; whatever its demerits, it got results.) When she could not speak a word, he rushed off in vexation, but he returned, and when his apprenticeship was over, they were married, and he set up, on borrowed money, as a saddler himself.

One day Peale journeyed to Norfolk for leather supplies and beheld the first paintings he had ever seen. In the unpublished autobiography that he got together from his diaries many years later, written in an archaic third person, he describes the effect of this experience. The paintings were miserable.

"Had they been better, perhaps they would not have led Peale to the idea of attempting anything in that way, but rather have smothered this faint spark of Genius. . . . The idea of making Pictures having now taken possession of his mind, as soon as he could he begins to try at a Landscape which was much praised by his companions. Next he began a portrait of himself, with a Clock taken to pieces before him, next his Wife's portrait, his Brothers and Sisters. . . . These beginnings were thought a good deal of, and Peale was applyed to by Captain Maybury to draw his and his Lady's portraits, and with some intreaty he at last undertook them, and for which he was to receive 10 pounds, and this gave the first idea to Peale that he possibly might do better by painting than with his other trades. . . ."

With his usual optimism, Peale at once advertised himself as a sign painter in addition to his other endeavors. He went to Philadelphia to buy paints and paid a timid call on a real artist, whom he found, rather inauspiciously, being hustled off by the sheriff for debt. Back home, he offered "one of his best saddles, with its complete furniture" to the artist John Hesselius 'if, in return, he might be permitted to watch him at work on a picture. Hesselius was agreeable, and even painted half a face so that Peale could fill in the rest.

Things did not go well for long with the new family, however. Peale's partner in his saddle business absconded with the cash; then his noisy espousal of the radical side in local politics so irritated his Tory creditors that they descended on him with writs. To avoid imprisonment for debt, Peale fled Annapolis with his wife, and when the sheriff still pursued, he sailed alone in a ship belonging to his brother-in-law to Massachusetts. The exile lasted a year and turned out to be a blessing in disguise. Peale studied for a while with Copley in Boston, and seemed so promising by the time his affairs were put in order and he returned home that a group of 11 wealthy Marylanders, headed by Charles Carroll of Carrollton, raised 81 guineas to send Peale to London to study under the great Benjamin West. Leaving his young wife again, the grateful Peale embarked, in 1766, on a ship which was, to his intense satisfaction, carrying back a cargo of tea that no one had been able to land in the rebellious colonies.

For two years he studied hard under the kindly West, and passed from his primitive colonial methods to a more refined style. In 1769, Peale returned to Maryland, clutching a bundle of painter's supplies and a huge, stilted canvas for his patrons, showing William Pitt in Roman robes orating in the West manner, but the artist himself was arrayed in the colonial clothes, now tattered, he had worn when he left. Patriotically, he would buy nothing in England.

From now on, Peale was to make his living in art, traveling the countryside in Virginia, Maryland, Delaware, and Pennsylvania, painting the gentry in a polished realistic style few of them had ever seen before. In 1776, at the beginning of the war, Peale took his growing family to live permanently in Philadelphia.

Caught up in the excitement of the Revolution, Peale, his friend David Rittenhouse, and his brother-in-law Nathaniel Ramsay made gunpowder at home, and Peale devised a kind of telescopic sight that unfortunately blacked his eye with its recoil the first time he fired the gun on which it was mounted. He joined the militia, and the company quickly elected him lieutenant, and later captain. And when Washington, after losing the New York campaign, began to fall back through New Jersey, and Philadelphia filled with alarm at the approach of Cornwallis, Peale raised a company of 81 and took to the field. His brother James and brother-in-law Ramsay were in the regular Continental Army; Peale was distressed to meet them, haggard and worn in defeat. He took a vigorous part in the campaigns around Trenton and Princeton and made the Delaware Crossing; he was on hand for the next campaign when the British, rallying from their defeats in New Jersey, approached and took Philadelphia from the south.

By modern standards, by *any* standards, Peale was a peculiar soldier. Discipline was alien to his nature. His main concern always seemed to be his men, and no body of troops ever had a commander who took their well-being more to heart. He did the foraging, and a lot of the cooking. He doctored his men and, when their boots wore out, procured hides and made them all moccasins by hand with cozy linings of fur. When there was nothing else to do, he painted miniatures of the high officers; he had conceived the idea that he should record, for later exhibition, the great men of the Revolution.

Washington seems to have crossed his path often, and once invited him to dinner. But in riding about searching for clean linen to wear at the occasion, Peale got so far away from headquarters that he failed to show up.

Peale was brave enough and served under fire, but he was not cut to the military measure. Once he came upon some retreating militia and, brandishing his sword as heroes do in romances, tried to rally them. But no one paid any attention, and Peale, having shouted himself hoarse, prudently joined the retreat.

After the tumult of the war, Peale turned to something new. For some time he had given floor space in his home picture gallery to a few old bones, gigantic in size, that had been presented to him as curiosities. One day Ramsay dropped in to see them and bluntly gave it as his opinion that, while a few people might like paintings, things like these bones

Washington's victory at Trenton and Princeton was painted by the elder Peale in 1779. Aided by his brother James, he made more than 20 similar canvases for clients all over the world.

would really bring crowds. Peale agreed enthusiastically.

What began shortly after the Revolution as a picture gallery behind his house at Third and Lombard Streets in Philadelphia, with a few curiosities exhibited here and there, grew into a never-before-equaled collection of birds, animals, and reptiles, arranged according to the classical order of Linnaeus, handsomely mounted and stuffed by Peale and his family. Many he had caught himself, with gun and bag. Others were contributed by his friends. (Franklin once sent him the corpse of his French angora cat and Washington some dead pheasants. Jefferson shipped him specimens brought back by the Lewis and Clark expedition.) That other animal, man (anticipating Darwin, Peale was sure of some relationship with monkeys), was represented not only by Peale's rows of portraits but by elaborate life-size waxworks of the various races.

Peale took his duties seriously. He placed all his specimens in natural surroundings, part stage set, part painted backdrop. (A hundred years ahead of his time, he had invented the "habitat" group.) There were, in addition, displays of minerals, of insects, and all branches of natural history; 100,000 items altogether, including the trigger finger of an executed murderer. A live eagle screamed in the rafters; the first complete mastodon skeleton ever assembled stood in a place of honor. Peale, who thought it was a mammoth, had dug it up.

As the museum grew, it moved to Philosophical Hall and finally into the second story of Independence Hall, which cost Peale $400 a year rent but lent a quasi-official air to the enterprise. It was a lively, bustling place, with a daughter playing a big organ, the sons lecturing, and occasional exhibits of such strange things as "moving pictures," an elaborate animated mechanical device of Peale's. Anticipating Hollywood by some hundred years, he had contrived a group of moving stage sets, complete with music and sound effects. Night fell over Market Street; Satan's Palace, as described by Milton, gave off a fiery pageantry; the *Bonhomme Richard* approached the *Serapis* and took her captive. For this last production, wooden waves moved mechanically in the foreground while transparent moving curtains passed "clouds" over the scene. Holes appeared in the sails and, as night fell, the American ship sank and the victors sailed off. Mrs. Peale took tickets.

There was an air of fun and excitement that one never finds in the respectable hush of modern museums. Once a dinner was given inside the huge skeleton of the mastodon and toasts were drunk to peace, progress, and so forth—Peale, a teetotaler, abstaining.

Unaccustomed as they were to solvency, the Peales basked for years in comparative wealth as the museum prospered. Peale, stunned at first by Rachel's death in 1790, went courting again the next year, married a New Yorker named Betsy de Peyster, and added to his family. He supported the improvident Raphaelle, and sent Rembrandt and Rubens abroad. Widowed again in 1804, he presently married his third wife, the Quaker Hannah Moore. About 1809 he bought a country place he called Farm Persevere, and later Belfield, and here he undertook, for a time, scientific agriculture.

Eventually, Peale returned to Philadelphia, his museum, and his first love, painting. He traveled to Washington with his pretty and skillful nieces, painting celebrities and dining at the White House. Always he seemed to catch his subjects in a moment of lively awareness. And although he still lacked confidence in his ability to paint "history," he was recording it at every stroke.

Jack-of-all-trades and master of several, Charles Willson Peale was in many respects a boy who never grew up, as several of his contemporaries noted: He was a pacifist who never lost his love of bright uniforms, an idealist with the manner of a promoter, a moralist who loved a good time. Curious, noisy, and upright, he came as close as any man could to embodying the American spirit in all the joy and optimism of its youth.

Oliver Jensen, a former editor of American Heritage, *is the author of many articles on American history and several books, among them* Carrier War *and* American Album.

Volume 4
ENCYCLOPEDIC SECTION

The two-page reference guide below lists the entries by categories. The entries in this section supplement the subject matter covered in the text of this volume. A **cross-reference** (*see*) means that a separate entry appears elsewhere in this section. However, certain important persons and events mentioned here have individual entries in the Encyclopedic Section of another volume. Consult the Index in Volume 18.

AMERICAN STATESMEN AND POLITICIANS

John Adams	Nathaniel Macon
Fisher Ames	James Madison
Joel Barlow	James Monroe
Aaron Burr	Gouverneur Morris
George Clinton	Samuel Osgood
Jonathan Dayton	Harrison Gray Otis
Oliver Ellsworth	William Paterson
Albert Gallatin	Timothy Pickering
Elbridge Gerry	Charles Cotesworth Pinckney
Alexander Hamilton	Edmund Randolph
Andrew Jackson	John Rutledge
John Jay	Roger Sherman
Thomas Jefferson	Daniel D. Tompkins
Rufus King	John Trumbull
William Maclay	George Washington

EUROPEAN LEADERS

Charles IV (Spain)	Louis Philippe (France)
Edmond Charles Genet (France)	Napoleon Bonaparte (France)
	Charles Maurice de Talleyrand (France)

EXPLORATION AND EXPANSION

Harman Blennerhassett	Little Turtle
Aaron Burr	Louisiana Purchase
George Rogers Clark	Northwest Ordinance
Battle of Fallen Timbers	Ordinance of 1785
John Ledyard	Treaty of San Ildefonso

FOREIGN RELATIONS

Convention of 1800
Embargo Act
Jay's Treaty

Macon's Bill No. 2
Non-Importation Act
Non-Intercourse Act
XYZ Affair

MILITARY DEVELOPMENTS

War with Algeria
William Bainbridge
Barbary Wars
Sir Isaac Brock
Constitution
Henry Dearborn
Stephen Decatur
William Eaton
Fort Dearborn
Edmund Pendleton Gaines
Isaac Hull
William Hull
Andrew Jackson

Jean Laffite
James Lawrence
Horatio Nelson
Battle of New Orleans
Sir Edward Pakenham
Peace of Ghent
Oliver Hazard Perry
Edward Preble
Sir George Prevost
Robert Ross
Tecumseh
Tenskwatawa
Tripolitan War
William Winder

POLITICAL DEVELOPMENTS

Bill of Rights
Connecticut Compromise
Constitution of the United States
electoral college
The Federalist Papers
French Revolution
Hartford Convention

Naturalization and Alien Acts
New Jersey Plan
Sedition Act
Shays' Rebellion
Virginia Plan
Washington's Farewell Address
Whiskey Rebellion

THE PRESIDENCY

John Adams
Thomas Jefferson
Dolley Madison
James Madison

James Monroe
Monticello
Mount Vernon
George Washington
Washington, D.C.

THOUGHT AND CULTURE

American Philosophical Society
Benjamin Banneker
Joel Barlow
Charles Brockden Brown
Abel Buell
George Rogers Clark
John Fenno
Robert Fulton
Albert Gallatin

Thomas Jefferson
Francis Scott Key
Pierre Charles L'Enfant
Charles Willson Peale
David Rittenhouse
The Star-Spangled Banner
Gilbert Stuart
John Trumbull
Noah Webster
Alexander Wilson

A

ADAMS, John (1735–1826). The major accomplishment of the second President of the United States was to negotiate a treaty with France (*see* **Convention of 1800**) that prevented open warfare between the two nations. His determination to make peace met stiff opposition in Congress and finally caused the downfall of the Federalist Party. Adams became President after serving two terms as Vice-President under **George Washington** (*see*) and serving America as a diplomat abroad. Born in Braintree (now Quincy), Massachusetts, Adams went to Harvard College and became a lawyer in 1758. Six years later, he married Abigail Smith (1744–1818). Although opposed to the restrictive British Stamp Act of 1765, he risked his popularity among his fellow Bostonians by skillfully defending nine British soldiers accused of murder in the Boston Massacre of 1770. Adams became a leading spokesman for American independence while serving as a delegate (1774–1777) to the First and Second Continental Congresses. He was on the committee that drafted the Declaration of Independence and was one of its signers. After a year abroad as commissioner to France, he was instrumental in drawing up the Massachusetts state constitution in 1779. The following year, he returned to Europe as minister to the Netherlands. He secured a loan and a commercial treaty with Holland in 1782 and then took part in the final talks that led to the Treaty of Paris, which ended the Revolutionary War against Britain in 1783. He later served as minister to Britain (1785–1788). Adams'

two terms as Vice-President (1789–1797) were troubled by conflicts with **Alexander Hamilton** (*see*), a fellow Federalist, and **Thomas Jefferson** (*see*), a political rival. Their clashes continued during his term as President (1797–1801) and severely hampered his administration. Soon after assuming office, Adams attempted to improve America's deteriorating relationship with France by sending a three-member commission to secure a commercial treaty with France. The mission was a failure (*see* **XYZ Affair**), and most Federalists and many Democratic-Republicans like Jefferson wanted war with France. Naval warfare ensued after 1798, and Congress took preparatory measures for declaring war. Adams, on his own, appointed another commission to go to France. This mission succeeded in negotiating the Convention of 1800, which restored peaceful relations with France. However, Adams' refusal to go to war caused a split in the Federalist Party, and Jefferson, a Democratic-Republican, was elected President in 1800. Adams then retired. He died on July 4, 1826, the same day on which Jefferson died. His son, John Quincy Adams (1767–1848), had been elected sixth President of the United States 18 months before. Of the first seven Presidents, only Adams and his son were not reelected.

ALGERIA, War with. *See* **Barbary Wars.**

AMERICAN PHILOSOPHICAL SOCIETY. The nation's oldest scholarly society was founded in Philadelphia in 1743 by Benjamin Franklin (1706–1790) "for the promotion of useful knowledge among the British plantations in America." The society

John Adams

was small and inactive until 1769, when Franklin took over as president. By 1771, 241 distinguished scientists, statesmen, public servants, and scholars from America and Europe belonged to it. The society's first publication, *Transactions,* which was started in 1769, became an important scientific document throughout the world. Franklin was succeeded as president in 1797 by **David Rittenhouse** (*see*). In 1801, another member, **Charles Willson Peale** (*see*), convinced President **Thomas Jefferson** (*see*) to allocate funds for the excavation of a recently discovered mastodon. Jefferson's enemies subsequently dubbed him Mr. Mammoth (*see p. 297*). The Philosophical Society's library is one of the oldest in the country. It houses a significant collection of Americana, including letters of Franklin and records of the Lewis and Clark expedition (1804–1806). Its membership is now limited to 500 persons.

AMES, Fisher (1758–1808). An eloquent orator, Ames was instrumental in securing Congressional approval of **Jay's Treaty** (*see*) with Britain in 1796. Ames was born in Massachusetts and graduated from Harvard when he was 16. He became a lawyer in 1781, but his reputation was based on his writings. A Federalist, Ames believed that America needed an aristocracy to govern it. He served four terms in Congress (1789–1797), becoming a chief spokesman for New England merchants who were opposed to declaring war on Britain. Despite ill health, Ames delivered the crucial speech in the House in favor of ratifying Jay's Treaty. His eloquence was so impressive that opponents immediately asked for an adjournment to break the spell his voice had cast. Ames retired in 1797. He served briefly on the governor's council of Massachusetts (1799–1801) but declined the presidency of Harvard because of ill health.

B

BAINBRIDGE, William (1774–1833). Bainbridge, a hero of the War of 1812, went to sea at the age of 15 and within four years became a captain in the merchant service. In 1798, he entered the United States Navy. That same year, during diplomatic difficulties with France, his ship was captured and he was imprisoned briefly. In 1800, prior to the Tri-politan War (*see* **Barbary Wars**), Bainbridge was ordered to deliver the tribute payments to Algiers for the protection of United States shipping. It was on this trip that the Algerian ruler forced Bainbridge to sail under a foreign flag on a diplomatic mission to the sultan of Turkey. Bainbridge resented this assignment. "I hope I may never again be sent to Algiers with *tribute*," he later wrote, "unless I am authorized to deliver it from the mouth of our cannon." Three years later, after the war had broken out, his ship, the *Philadelphia,* ran aground off Tripoli, and he and his men were held prisoner until 1805. To prevent the Tripolitans from using the ship, **Stephen Decatur** (*see*) sneaked into the harbor of Tripoli in 1804 and set fire to the vessel. Bainbridge commanded a squadron during the War of 1812. He commanded the *Constitution* (*see*) in her victory over the British frigate *Java* (*see pp. 324–325*), even though he was wounded twice during the battle. Before retiring from the navy in 1821, he was captain of the *Independence* and subsequently succeeded Decatur in command of American naval units in the Mediterranean.

BANNEKER, Benjamin (1736–1806). Banneker, a free black from Maryland, helped **Pierre L'Enfant** (*see*) survey the land that had been chosen for the nation's capital, **Washington, D.C.** (*see*). As a youth, Banneker displayed unusual mechanical ability and reputedly constructed a clock out of wood. A Quaker neighbor lent him surveying equipment and astronomical texts. He studied so carefully that he was able to predict an eclipse of the sun. In 1789, L'Enfant was appointed to design the plans for the new federal capital, and at the suggestion of **Thomas Jefferson** (*see*), he asked Banneker to help him survey the sites for the capital's principal buildings. In 1791, Banneker published the first of a series of almanacs that so impressed Jefferson that he sent it to a prominent member of the Academy of Sciences in Paris as an illustration of black talent.

BARBARY WARS. The Barbary Wars encompassed two conflicts, the Tripolitan War (1801–1805) and the War with Algeria (1815). Aside from one land campaign, the Tripolitan War was fought at sea off the coast of North Africa. Since the 16th century, the rulers of the Barbary States—Tripoli, Algiers, Morocco, and Tunis—had lived by plunder, receiving part of all the goods captured by local pirates. These corsairs cruised the Mediterranean, seizing merchant vessels. They kept the cargoes and held the crews for ransom or sold them as slaves. To protect themselves from such attacks, the European powers, and later the United States, made treaties with the Barbary rulers and paid large sums of money each year as tribute. However, the pirates often disregarded these agreements and raided supposedly protected ships. In spite of large payments made by the United States—which in 1795 paid almost $1,000,000 in tribute—Barbary pirates frequently attacked American trading ships. The Tripolitan War began in 1801, when the United States refused to grant Tripoli's demand for increased tribute. Tripoli subsequently declared war. The American government dispatched two naval squadrons, the first commanded by Richard Dale (1756–1826) and the second

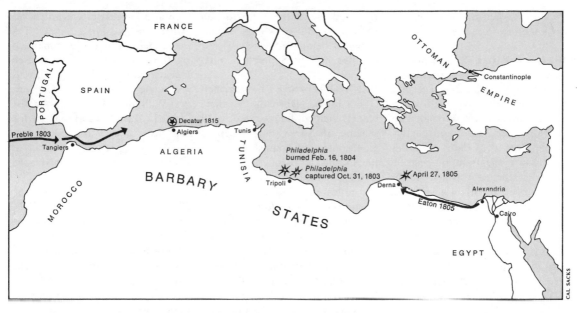

American naval squadrons put down the threat to merchant ships from the Barbary pirates of North Africa.

by Richard V. Morris (1768–1815), but both failed to subdue the pirates. In 1803, a third squadron under **Edward Preble** (*see*) was sent to North African waters. The appearance of this fleet outside the Moroccan port of Tangiers in November of that year was enough to keep Morocco from joining Tripoli in the war. It also stopped Morocco's interference with American commerce by frightening its ruler into renewing his treaty with the United States. During August and September of 1804, Preble blockaded the port of Tripoli and made five unsuccessful attempts to capture it. He was relieved of his command soon afterward, but the blockade was continued. Finally, an American land force, led by **William Eaton** (*see*) and supported by a small naval unit, captured the Tripolitan port of Derna on April 27, 1805. A peace treaty was subsequently signed on June 4, 1805. Tripoli renounced the right to collect further tribute and ransomed

the prisoners it held for $60,000. The United States continued to pay tribute to the other Barbary States, and, as before, the pirates continued to raid American shipping, especially at the outset of the War of 1812 between America and Britain. Algiers then demanded further tribute, and when refused, declared war on the United States. The American government did not take action until the war with Britain ended in 1815. In the spring of that year, Congress sent a squadron of 10 ships under **Stephen Decatur** (*see*) to the Mediterranean. Decatur captured two Algerian warships in mid-June and sailed into the harbor of Algiers on June 30, 1815. He forced its ruler to sign a treaty that ended the raids on American shipping as well as the payment of tribute. Later that summer, Decatur negotiated similar treaties with the rulers of Tripoli and Tunis and required them to release all Christians who had been enslaved.

BARLOW, Joel (1754–1812). Barlow, an American poet and statesman, was a Yale student who, during his summer vacation, took part in the Battle of Long Island on August 27, 1776. He first achieved national fame when his nine-volume epic poem, *The Vision of Columbus,* was published in 1787. Barlow left for Europe the next year and eventually settled in France. In 1795, he was appointed American consul to Algiers, where he negotiated an uneasy peace with the Barbary States (*see* **Barbary Wars**). Barlow returned to America in 1805 and in 1811 was sent to France to negotiate a commercial agreement with **Napoleon** (*see*). They never met. The French emperor was engaged in his disastrous attack on Russia at the time and was in full retreat before Barlow arrived in Poland for a meeting. While he was waiting futilely for Napoleon, Barlow wrote his last and best poem, "Advice to a Raven in Russia December 1812." A few weeks later, on December

24, Barlow died of pneumonia in a village near Cracow.

BILL OF RIGHTS. The first 10 amendments to the **Constitution** (*see*), known as the Bill of Rights, deal with the individual liberties of citizens. These amendments guarantee the freedom of religion, of speech, and of the press. They also assure the right of peaceful assembly, the right to petition the government to correct grievances, the right to a speedy and fair trial, and the right to keep and bear arms. In addition, they protect against unwarranted search and seizure, double jeopardy, excessive bail and fines, "cruel and unusual" punishment, the private obligation to quarter soldiers, and other violations of personal liberty. Sponsored by **James Madison** (*see*), the Bill of Rights became part of the Constitution on December 15, 1791, after a long battle between followers of **Alexander Hamilton** and **Thomas Jefferson** (*see both*). The Constitutional Convention had adjourned in 1787 without incorporating a specific statement of individual rights. Hamilton argued that because the Constitution was the political instrument of the people themselves —the document begins, "We the people . . ."—the spelling out of individual rights was unnecessary. His opponents, however, demanded a detailed listing of fundamental liberties. They feared that once a strong central government had assumed control, it would claim for itself the power to decide what were the "rights" of its subjects. Several politically powerful states—notably New York, Massachusetts, and Virginia—agreed to ratify the Constitution only after assurances had been given that a well-defined Bill of Rights would be a basic part of the law of the land. Like the Constitution proper, the Bill of Rights is continually being interpreted and clarified by the Supreme Court.

BLENNERHASSETT, Harman (1765–1831). Harman Blennerhassett helped finance the bold scheme of **Aaron Burr** (*see*) to gain control of Spanish lands in the Southwest. Blennerhassett, an Irishman, was born in England and educated in Dublin, where he became a lawyer. Independently wealthy, he immigrated in 1796 to the United States, where he purchased part of an island, now known as Blennerhassett Island, in the Ohio River near Parkersburg, in present-day West Virginia. There he lived elegantly and pursued cultural and scientific interests. He met Burr in 1805 and became involved in an alleged plan to seize territories in the Southwest and Mexico and to establish an independent nation. When Burr was accused of treason and arrested in 1807, Blennerhassett was also arrested, and his lavish estate was looted by local militiamen. Burr was acquitted, and Blennerhassett was never brought to trial. He tried unsuccessfully to regain his fortune on a cotton plantation in Mississippi and practiced law in Montreal after 1819. Blennerhassett returned to Britain in 1822 and died on the Isle of Guernsey.

BROCK, Sir Isaac (1769–1812). Known as the hero of Upper Canada, this professional soldier led British forces in Canada until his death in battle during the War of 1812. Brock was both provisional lieutenant governor and commander of all British forces in what was then called Upper Canada. At the outset of the war, he organized the militia of the province and successfully warded off American invasion attempts. Together with Indians commanded by the Shawnee chief **Tecumseh** (*see*), he captured Detroit without a struggle from the American general **William Hull** (*see*) on August 16, 1812. Brock was knighted for this feat. He was killed two months later at the Battle of Queenston Heights on the Niagara frontier.

BROWN, Charles Brockden (1771–1810). This Philadelphia-born author was the first American novelist to win an international reputation. After a short legal career, Brown decided in 1793 to become a writer, an occupation that was then considered a hobby or a pastime. He wrote his best-known novels after settling in New York in 1798. They were similar to the Gothic horror stories that were then popular in England. His novels had American settings and usually pitted an innocent youth against a villain. In his novel *Ormond,* published in 1799, Brown included material from his observations of a yellow-fever epidemic that ravaged Philadelphia in 1793 and forced his family to flee to the country. A second novel published in 1799, *Edgar Huntly,* takes place on the American frontier. Unable to support himself as a novelist, Brown returned to Philadelphia in 1801, where he made his living as a magazine editor and merchant until his death.

BUELL, Abel (1742–1822). A printer, typefounder, silversmith, and engraver, Buell designed and cast the first American-made printing type in 1769. Fifteen years later, he compiled and published the earliest large-scale map of the United States printed in America (*see p. 277*). It included territories ceded by Britain in the Treaty of Paris, which officially ended the Revolution in 1783. The map measured 41 by 46 inches.

BURR, Aaron (1756–1836). On July 11, 1804, in a duel at Weehawken, New Jersey, Vice-President Aaron Burr fatally wounded **Alexander Hamilton** (*see*), former Secretary of the Treasury. Burr's revenge on his lifelong enemy cost him his reputation and his political career. Born in Newark, New Jersey, Burr came from a family of eminent churchmen. His father was a founder and president of the College of New Jersey (now Princeton University). His maternal grandfather was Jonathan Edwards (1703–1758), the most famous Puritan preacher of his day. After graduating from the College in 1772 at the age of 16, Burr studied theology for a time and then law. During the Revolution, he served under Benedict Arnold (1741–1801) in the campaign against Quebec in the first winter of the war. He then became a staff aide to **George Washington** (*see*) but was soon transferred to other duties because of his arrogance. Ill health forced him to resign from the army in 1779. In 1783, Burr began practicing law in New York City and soon became a bitter rival of Hamilton. A Democratic-Republican, he served as attorney general of New York (1789–1791) and then United States Senator (1791–1797). In the Presidential election of 1800, Burr, a candidate for Vice-President, received the same number of electoral votes as his party's Presidential candidate, **Thomas Jefferson** (*see*). As a result, the choice of a new President was made by the House of Representatives. Hamilton, a Federalist, distrusted Burr more than he disliked

Aaron Burr

Jefferson, and he used his influence to defeat Burr, who then became Vice-President. Burr's ambitions were again thwarted in 1804, when Hamilton worked to defeat his nomination for governor of New York. Burr subsequently challenged Hamilton to a duel and killed him. Burr's hunger for wealth and power then took him westward. He conspired with General James Wilkinson (1757–1825) and **Harman Blennerhassett** (*see*) to seize control of part of Spanish America and create a new nation with himself as ruler. Arrested and charged with treason in 1807, Burr was tried at Richmond, Virginia. He was acquitted on a legal technicality involving the constitutional interpretation of treason. Burr next went to Europe, where he spent four years (1808–1812) trying to persuade first the English and then **Napoleon** (*see*) to back his schemes for an empire. In 1812, he returned to America and practiced law in New York until his death in 1836.

C

CHARLES IV (1748–1819). Charles IV, an ineffectual king of Spain (1788–1808), ceded the vast Louisiana Territory to France by the secret Treaty of San Ildefonso in 1800. France had given the territory to Spain 38 years earlier, but **Napoleon** (*see*) wanted it back as part of a colonial empire he intended to build in the West Indies and North America. The treaty was part of a series of secret agreements, beginning in 1796, that allied Spain and France against Great Britain. In return for Louisiana, Napoleon placed Charles IV's son-in-law on the throne of the newly created kingdom of Etruria in Italy. However, diplomatic problems involved in the land transfer (*see pp. 335–337*) and Napoleon's need for money to finance his military adventures led him to sell the Louisiana Territory to the United States in 1803 (*see* **Louisiana Purchase**). In 1808, after Napoleon had invaded Spain, Charles IV was forced to abdicate his throne and was replaced by his son, Ferdinand VII (1784–1833). Napoleon captured the royal family and held them prisoner in France until 1814.

Charles IV

CLARK, George Rogers (1752–1818). A native Virginian with little formal schooling, Clark took a leading part in the settlement of present-day Kentucky, defending its inhabitants against Indian raids organized by the British. During the early part of the Revolution, Clark captured a number of British-held towns, including Vincennes in present-day Indiana. As a result, he was able to prevent the British from gaining control of the Old Northwest, which included territory north of the Ohio River. After the war, Clark protected this area against Indian assaults. Although he successfully defended Vincennes in 1786, he got into difficulties for seizing supplies to feed his troops and was never again asked to serve the government. He later became involved in several attempts by the French to recapture the Louisiana Territory from Spain. Clark believed that the mysterious earthen mounds found in the Ohio and Mississippi Valleys were built by the ancestors of the Indians living in that region. His theory, not published until more than 40

George Rogers Clark

years after his death, is now accepted by modern archaeologists. Clark's brother was the famous explorer William Clark (1770–1838).

CLINTON, George (1739–1812). Seven times the governor of New York and known as the father of his state, Clinton served twice as Vice-President of the United States. An open advocate of independence from Britain, he was a brigadier general in both the New York militia and the Continental Army. Although courageous, he was not a competent commander, and he failed to prevent the British from capturing Fort Montgomery or burning Esopus, New York, in the fall of 1777. He became the first governor of New York that year and served six successive terms until 1795. He vigorously opposed ratification of the **Constitution** (*see*) because he believed it would diminish his state's power. Clinton served a seventh term as governor in 1800. He became Vice-President under **Thomas Jefferson** (*see*) in 1805 and again under **James Madison** (*see*) in 1809. He died in office three years later. One of his last important acts while presiding in the Senate was to break a tie on rechartering the Bank of the United States by voting against it.

CONNECTICUT COMPROMISE. Also known as the Great Compromise, the Connecticut Compromise of July 16, 1787, resolved one of the major deadlocks of the Constitutional Convention —namely, how the states would be represented in the federal legislature. The **Virginia Plan** (*see*) had favored the larger states by proposing a two-chamber legislature in which the states would be represented according to popula-

tion. The smaller states reacted by supporting the **New Jersey Plan** (*see*), which advocated a one-chamber legislature in which each state would have equal representation. The Connecticut Compromise, put forward by **Roger Sherman** (*see*) of Connecticut on June 11, 1787, solved the problem by proposing that the states have equal representation in the Senate and representation according to population in the House of Representatives. After some amendments, this plan was accepted.

CONSTITUTION. The *Constitution* was one of six large frigates authorized by Congress in 1794 to meet the growing threat of naval warfare with both France and the Barbary pirates (*see* **Barbary Wars**). Commissioned in 1797, she was more than 200 feet in length and was designed to carry 44 heavy guns, though this was later increased to 55. In the summer of 1804, the *Constitution,* under the command of **Edward Preble** (*see*), took part in five attacks on Tripoli in North Africa. When the War of 1812 began, **Isaac Hull** (*see*) took the ship to sea without orders and destroyed the British frigate *Guerriere* on August 19, 1812. It was the first important American naval victory of the War of 1812. During this battle, a sailor on the *Constitution* gave her the nickname Old Ironsides when he saw a British shot bounce harmlessly off her hull and shouted, "Her sides are made of iron!" Four months later, under **William Bainbridge** (*see*), the *Constitution* sank the British warship *Java* (*see pp. 324–325*). Slated for scrapping by the Navy Department in 1830, the *Constitution* was saved by the public sentiment aroused by Oliver Wendell Holmes' poem "Old Ironsides" (1830). She is now moored in the Boston Navy Yard and is open to the public.

CONSTITUTION OF THE UNITED STATES.

The Constitution, the oldest written national charter still in effect in the world, is a document that contains the basic laws and principles that govern the United States. It was drawn up at Philadelphia between May and September of 1787, when 55 delegates from 12 colonies (Rhode Island did not participate) met to revise the original charter of the United States, the Articles of Confederation (*see pp. 285–290*). **George Washington** (*see*) presided over the deliberations. Finding the Articles too weak and inconsistent to ensure national unity, the delegates devised an entirely new framework of government, with a powerful central authority. Before the final draft was signed by 39 delegates on September 17, many compromises had been made. A major conflict developed over representation in the legislative branch. The **Virginia Plan** (*see*), or "large-state" proposal, was countered by the **New Jersey Plan** (*see*), which sought to protect the interests of the less populous states. The **Connecticut Compromise** (*see*) resolved the matter by giving Congress its present two-chamber structure, with the House membership based on state population and membership in the Senate equally divided. Other hotly debated issues—such as slavery, taxation, and the control of commerce—were also settled by compromise. A chief feature of the Constitution was its provision for the "separation of powers" among Congress, the President, and the federal courts. This system of "checks and balances" has pre-

vented any one branch of government or political faction from gaining dictatorial power. The Constitution was officially adopted on June 21, 1788, after nine of the original 13 states had ratified it. It went into effect on March 4, 1789. The Constitution originally consisted of a short Preamble, or introduction, and seven Articles. Articles I, II, and III describe the organization and functions of Congress, the President and Vice-President, and the Supreme Court and judicial system. Article IV makes all states equal to one another and provides for the admission of new states. Article V outlines the procedure for amending the Constitution. Article VI tells how the Constitution "shall be the supreme Law of the Land" and forbids any religious test for government officeholders. Article VII describes the procedure that was employed to ratify the Constitution. One of the main strengths of the Constitution is its flexibility. Since it became effective in 1789, 25 amendments have been added to it. The first 10 are known as the **Bill of Rights** (*see*), which guarantees, among other things, the freedom of religion and of speech and an uncensored press.

CONVENTION OF 1800.

Also known as the Treaty of Morfontaine, this agreement ended two years of undeclared naval warfare between the United States and France. The treaty, which was signed on September 30, 1800, went into effect on December 21, 1801. It was the result of the determination of President **John Adams** (*see*) to end hostilities by diplomacy. The French, who were at war with Britain, were angry over **Jay's Treaty** (*see*) of 1794 between America and Britain, which, among other things, opened

American ports to the British. Contrary to the wishes of a pro-war faction in Congress, Adams finally appointed a commission to negotiate with French diplomats. He did so only after the French foreign minister, **Talleyrand** (*see*), assured him that an American minister would be treated with respect. The convention released the United States from its Revolutionary War alliance of 1778 with France and led to renewed commercial activity between the two nations.

D

DAYTON, Jonathan (1760–1824).

Dayton was the youngest member of the Constitutional Convention

Jonathan Dayton

in 1787. The 27-year-old New Jersey lawyer attended in place of his father, Elias Dayton (1737–1807), a former revolutionary general. Young Dayton served with his father during the war. Afterward, he was elected four times to the House of Representatives (1791–1799) and once to the Senate (1799–1805). Dayton, who held about 250,000 acres of land in what is now Ohio, was a friend of **Aaron Burr** (*see*) and was indicted with Burr for treason in 1807. Dayton was never brought to trial, but his career in national politics was ruined. He later served in the New Jersey legislature (1814–1815).

DEARBORN, Henry (1751–1829). A veteran of the Revolution, Dearborn commanded American forces along the Canadian border at the outset of the War of 1812 but was recalled after a year because of his ineptness. Born in New Hampshire, Dearborn studied to be a doctor. During the Revolution, he took part in several major battles and was on George Washington's staff at the triumphant siege of Yorktown in 1781. Dearborn represented Massachusetts for two terms in the House of Representatives (1793–1797) and was later appointed Secretary of War (1801–1809) by President **Thomas Jefferson** (*see*). Jefferson's successor, **James Madison** (*see*), appointed Dearborn the senior major general in the army when the war with Britain started in 1812. Dearborn's mismanagement of campaigns against the British general **Sir Isaac Brock** (*see*) led to his recall. When Madison tried to appoint Dearborn Secretary of War in 1815, so many objections were raised that Madison withdrew the nomination. Dearborn later served as minister to Portugal (1822–1824).

DECATUR, Stephen (1779–1820). One of America's leading naval heroes, Decatur first won fame in the Tripolitan War (*see* **Barbary Wars**). Born in Maryland, he joined the American navy in 1798 and was promoted from midship-

man to acting lieutenant in May, 1799. In November, 1803, Decatur, as commander of the *Enterprise,* captured the ketch *Mastico* off Tripoli. He then suggested that the ship, renamed the *Intrepid,* be used to destroy the American frigate *Philadelphia,* which had been captured by the Tripolitans. This Decatur accomplished on the night of February 16, 1804, in a surprise attack that the famed English admiral, **Horatio Nelson** (*see*), reputedly described as "the most bold and daring act of the age." After the outbreak of the War of 1812, Decatur, now captain of the *United States,* captured the British frigate *Macedonian* off the Moroccan coast near Madeira on October 25, 1812 (*see pp. 322–323*). His last active service was an expedition to the Barbary States in the summer of 1815. He forced the rulers of Algiers, Tunis, and Tripoli to cease their attacks on American shipping in the Mediterranean. After his return home, Decatur was honored at numerous dinners, and during one he made his famous toast, "Our country! In her intercourse with foreign nations may she always be in the right; but our country, right or wrong." In November, 1815, Decatur was appointed to the Board of Navy Commissioners. He was killed in a duel with James Barron (1769–1851), a suspended officer whom he had refused to reinstate.

E

EATON, William (1764–1811). Eaton, a Connecticut-born diplomat, led a decisive expedition of the Tripolitan War (*see* **Barbary Wars**). In 1804, Eaton proposed to Congress that Tripoli's hostile pasha, Yusuf Caramanli, be re-

placed by his exiled older brother, Hamet, who claimed the throne. Hamet promised to make peace with the United States. Eaton went to the Mediterranean and found the exiled Hamet in Egypt. He took him to Alexandria and recruited a force of about 370 men that included Greek mercenaries, Arab camel drivers, and seven United States marines under the command of Lieutenant Presley Neville O'Bannon (1776–1850). Eaton then marched this force 600 miles across the desert to the seaport town of Derna, the pasha's capital. On April 26, 1805, Eaton, supported by gunfire from three American ships in the harbor, stormed and captured the city. The Mameluke sword, still carried by marine officers, is patterned on a sword presented to Lieutenant O'Bannon by Hamet after the battle. Eaton, who held the city until Yusuf Caramanli began peace negotiations with the United States, was recalled before a treaty had been signed. The settlement permitted Yusuf to remain on the throne. In 1807, Eaton was elected to the Massachusetts legislature and served one term.

ELECTORAL COLLEGE. The President and Vice-President of the United States are chosen by a group of electors known as the electoral college. Each state has as many electors as it has Senators and Representatives. Hence, the electoral college has the same number of members as Congress. By law, no Presidential elector may be a Congressman or other federal officeholder. In the event that no Presidential candidate receives a majority of votes in the electoral college, the House of Representatives elects the President and the Senate chooses the Vice-President. The framers of the

Constitution (*see*) did not believe that a citizen was sufficiently informed or responsible to be entrusted with direct election of the President. Therefore, Article II, Section 1, of the Constitution directs each state to select its electors. In 1800, only five of the 16 states then in the Union chose electors by popular election. Today, all states pick electors by direct popular vote. It was originally believed that each elector would vote independently, according to his individual conscience and judgment. The framers of the Constitution did not foresee the development of political parties, with their "slates" of electors all pledged beforehand to support the party candidate. This "general-ticket system" is now in effect in every state. Although the electoral college has come to be regarded as little more than a formality, many view this method of indirect election as undemocratic. Three candidates lost election to the Presidency in the electoral college, although they had won a plurality of the popular vote—**Andrew Jackson** (*see*) in 1824, Samuel Tilden (1814–1886) in 1876, and Grover Cleveland (1837–1908) in 1888. A number of proposals have been made in recent years to alter or abolish the electoral college in favor of direct Presidential elections.

ELLSWORTH, Oliver (1745–1807). Ellsworth was the second Chief Justice of the United States. Born in Connecticut, he became a lawyer in 1771. As a delegate to the Constitutional Convention of 1787, he was instrumental in drafting the **Connecticut Compromise** (*see*). One of the first two Senators from Connecticut, Ellsworth was chairman of the committee that organized the federal judiciary. He was appointed sec-

ond Chief Justice of the Supreme Court in 1796 when the Senate refused to confirm the nomination of **John Rutledge** (*see*). While on the Court, he was sent by President **John Adams** (*see*) to France with a commission to negotiate an end to the undeclared naval war with that nation (*see* **Convention of 1800**). Ellsworth took part in the peace talks, but the hardships of the journey had ruined his health. He resigned his post as Chief Justice in 1800 and retired to his home in Connecticut.

EMBARGO ACT. The Embargo Act of 1807 was part of the policy advocated by President **Thomas Jefferson** (*see*) to keep the United States from involvement in conflicts between England and France. The **Non-Importation Act** (*see*) of 1806 had failed to prevent the warring nations from harassing American trading vessels. After the British attacked the warship *Chesapeake* on June 22, 1807, some Americans wanted to declare war on England. However, Jefferson decided to try economic

reprisals and proposed the bill that was passed in Congress on December 22, 1807. The Embargo Act virtually cut off all foreign commerce by forbidding American ships to go abroad for 14 months. As a result, exports soon declined 75%, and imports dropped 50%. The new law, however, was bitterly opposed by both New England merchants, whose ships remained idle, and by Southern planters, who depended on selling their cotton to English manufacturers. Moreover, the act was impossible to enforce, and smuggling became widespread along the Canadian and Florida borders. The economic sanctions did not make England and France alter their policies. The Embargo Act was repealed in March, 1809, and succeeded by the **Non-Intercourse Act** (*see*).

F

FALLEN TIMBERS, Battle of. This battle, which took place on August 20, 1794, near present-day

Anthony Wayne leads the attack on the Miami Indians at Fallen Timbers.

Toledo, Ohio, was a decisive victory for American forces led by General Anthony Wayne (1745–1796), and it ended the Indian threat in the Northwest Territory. Although the Treaty of Paris in 1783 ceded the region northwest of the Ohio River to the United States, the British refused to give up control of their border forts and incited the Indians to attack the American settlers. In 1792, Wayne was given command of an army and ordered to negotiate with the Indians. However, the tribes, encouraged by recent victories and British support, refused to make peace. After the Indians, led by their chief, **Little Turtle** (*see*), attacked Fort Recovery in 1794, Wayne decided to retaliate. He led about 2,000 soldiers and 1,600 Kentucky volunteers to the mouth of the Maumee River, where about 1,300 Indian braves had assembled. The site was called Fallen Timbers because of the numerous fallen trees in the area, which served as a natural fortress. Wayne waited three days, until the Indians had exhausted their food supplies and had dispatched a hunting party to obtain game. He then attacked the 800 remaining braves, defeating them in a two-hour battle. As a result of the American victory, the British abandoned their outposts, and the Indians relinquished most of their Ohio lands to the United States in the Treaty of Greenville in 1795.

FEDERALIST PAPERS, THE.

This series of 77 essays was written to promote the ratification of the **Constitution** (*see*) by New York State. The majority were written by **Alexander Hamilton** and the rest by **James Madison** and **John Jay** (*see all*). They were first published in New York City newspapers from October, 1787,

A first edition of this American classic was sold for more than $1,000 in 1967.

to April, 1788, and later, with eight additional essays, in a two-volume book entitled *The Federalist*. The authors, in explaining the Constitution, discussed the potential dangers that might arise from undue foreign influence as well as disagreements between the individual states. They argued that a strong central authority was essential. Under the new Constitution, the authors said, one branch of government would check the power of the other two branches. Hence, the power of the nation would be balanced between the legislative, judicial, and executive branches. *The Federalist Papers* are considered among the most important works in the history of political thought.

FENNO, John

FENNO, John (1751–1798). After serving during the Revolution as secretary to General Artemas Ward (1727–1800), Fenno founded the *Gazette of the United States* in New York in 1789. The purpose of the newspaper was to spread "favorable sentiments of the federal Constitution and the Administration." He moved the *Gazette* to Philadelphia the following year. His publication, which never had a large circulation, strongly supported the Federalist Party, and **Alexander Hamilton** (*see*) was a frequent contributor of articles. On one occasion, Hamilton saved Fenno from bankruptcy by raising the money to pay his debts. The *Gazette* was published for two more years after he died of yellow fever in 1798.

FORT DEARBORN.

FORT DEARBORN. This fort, best remembered for the massacre in 1812 that occurred near it, guarded the Midwestern frontier for more than 30 years. Built in 1803 at the mouth of the Chicago River, the fort controlled the territory between Lake Michigan and the Mississippi River. Shortly after the outbreak of the War of 1812, **William Hull** (*see*), convinced that the isolated fort could not be supplied or properly defended, ordered its evacuation. On August 15, the small garrison and several women and children left the fort. After traveling about two miles, they were ambushed by a band of 500 Potawatomi Indians, who killed or captured the entire garrison and then burned the fort. It was rebuilt in 1816, and a small settlement grew up around it that eventually became the city of Chicago. Fort Dearborn was torn down in 1856, after the Indian threat was finally ended.

FRENCH REVOLUTION.

FRENCH REVOLUTION. The immediate causes of the French Revolution (1789–1799) were the intolerable burdens of taxation on the French people, social injustices, food shortages, and economic depression. An indirect cause was the American Revolution (1775–1783), which demonstrated that a determined people could successfully throw off an oppressive government. By the late 1780s, the French nation was nearly bankrupt. Louis XVI (1754–1793) was not able to cope with either his nation's financial plight or the mounting social conflict between the aristocracy, the peasants, and the merchants. As the revolution gathered headway, the king was forced to accept a representative National Assembly. He was also required to approve a declaration of individual rights and a constitution. Thus, the privileges of both the aristocracy and the Roman Catholic Church were ended. "Liberty, Equality, Fraternity" became the rallying cry of the revolutionaries. When the king dismissed his popular finance minister, Jacques Necker (1732–1804), a mob stormed the Bastille, a notorious prison in Paris, on July 14, 1789. The king recalled Necker, but the national situation continued to worsen. When Louis XVI attempted to flee in June, 1791, he was captured and imprisoned at Paris. He and his queen, Marie Antoinette (1775–1793), were tried for treason, and both were executed in 1793. For almost a decade, internal strife raged, as power passed from one political faction to another. Among the leaders who gained and then fell from power were Georges Jacques Danton (1759–1794), Louis de Saint-Just (1767–1794), and Maximilien de Robespierre (1758–1794). During the Reign of Terror (1793–1794), thousands died on the guillotine. The revolution ended, in the opinion of many historians, on November 9, 1799, when **Napoleon** (*see*) seized power. Although the French Revolution produced much bloodshed and ended in military dictatorship, it served to prod other governments in Europe into becoming more democratic.

FULTON, Robert (1765–1815). In August, 1807, Robert Fulton's steamboat, known to history as the *Clermont,* churned up the Hudson River from New York City to Albany and returned, averaging about five miles per hour. By thus demonstrating the efficiency of steam power for navigation, Fulton ushered in a new age of commerce and transportation. Fulton was born near Lancaster, Pennsylvania. The son of poor Irish immigrants, he received little education but showed a genius for mechanics and a gift for drawing. He learned gunsmithing from local craftsmen and invented a manually operated paddle wheel for boats. Between the ages of 17 and 21, Fulton earned his living painting portraits and landscapes in Philadelphia. He went to England in 1786 to study painting with Benjamin West (1738–1820) and remained abroad for 20 years. In England, his interest soon turned to engineering projects, especially canals and aqueducts. He invented a power shovel for digging canals and an inclined plane for raising and lowering canal boats. Other early inventions were machines for spinning flax, sawing marble, and making rope. Fulton moved to Paris in 1797 and for several years was mainly occupied with building and testing submarines, mines, and torpedoes. There he met the American minister to France, Robert R. Livingston (1746–1813), who held exclusive rights to steamboat navigation on the Hudson River. In 1802, Livingston agreed to back Fulton in constructing a commercially practical steamship. In 1806, after several years of experimentation, Fulton returned to the United States, where his efforts were rewarded the following year when the *Clermont*—referred to as Fulton's Folly by scoffers—successfully plied the Hudson. Although Fulton did not invent the steamboat, he was the first to engineer a workable model that efficiently

The French Revolution began when the Bastille in Paris was attacked.

In 1861, Fulton and his steamboat were commemorated in this drawing.

combined engine, boiler, paddle wheels, and hull. Fulton designed many other steam vessels before his death in 1815.

G

GAINES, Edmund Pendleton (1777–1849).

A career army officer, Gaines was awarded a gold medal by Congress for successfully commanding the defense of Fort Erie in 1814. In 1807, as a captain in the army, he arrested **Aaron Burr** (*see*) and was a witness against the former Vice-President at his conspiracy trial. During the War of 1812, Gaines was promoted to adjutant general and placed in command of Fort Erie, on the Canadian side of the Niagara River. In August, 1814, superior British forces launched a heavy attack, but Gaines' troops repulsed them. Gaines later fought in the Black Hawk War in 1832 and the Florida War in 1835. When the Mexican War broke out in 1846, Gaines was in command of the Western Department of the army but was removed on charges of insubordination. He was acquitted and later given command of the Eastern Department.

GALLATIN, Albert (1761–1849).

Gallatin was a financial genius who served as Secretary of the Treasury from 1801 to 1813 during the administrations of **Thomas Jefferson** and **James Madison** (*see both*). Born in Switzerland, Gallatin came to America in 1780 to seek his fortune. By 1788, he was active in Pennsylvania politics as a member of the Democratic-Republican Party, which supported states' rights over a strong central government. Gallatin was elected to the House of Representatives in 1795 and soon was recognized as the leader of the House's Democratic-Republican minority. His financial ability and support of Jefferson's policies led to his appointment as head of the

Albert Gallatin

Treasury in 1801. Gallatin's monetary plans were sound, and by 1807 he had considerably reduced the national debt, even though the Jefferson administration had spent $15,000,000 in 1803 for the **Louisiana Purchase** (*see*). Nevertheless, increased government expenses in the next few years, especially the costs involved in the War of 1812, made it difficult for him to carry out his fiscal policies. In 1813, Gallatin requested a diplomatic assignment and was sent to St. Petersburg, Russia. The following year, he played a crucial role in negotiating the **Peace of Ghent** (*see*), which ended the War of 1812. He later served as minister to France (1816–1823) and minister to Britain (1826–1827) before settling in New York City. Gallatin is often called the father of American ethnology because of his studies of American Indians.

GENET, Edmond Charles (1763–1834).

Citizen Genet, as he was called in the fashion of the **French Revolution** (*see*), was the first minister sent to America by the French Republic. Genet arrived in 1793, hoping to convince America to join France in its war against England. He also attempted to persuade American citizens to organize expeditions against Spanish Florida and tried to commission privateers to harass British ships off American shores (*see pp. 310–312*). When President **George Washington** (*see*) issued in 1793 a proclamation of neutrality, which stated that America would not involve itself in the war, Genet condemned Washington and dispatched the privateers. Washington finally asked the French government to recall Genet, and he was replaced in 1794. Afraid he would be executed if he returned to France, Genet moved instead to Long Island. He later married the daughter of New York's governor, **George Clinton** (*see*), and subsequently became an American citizen.

GERRY, Elbridge (1744–1814). A signer of the Declaration of Independence in 1776, Gerry was Vice-President of the United States from March 4, 1813, until his death on November 23, 1814. Although he was a delegate to the Constitutional Convention of 1787, he refused to sign the **Constitution** (*see*) because it did not contain a bill of rights. Gerry was born in Marblehead, Massachusetts, the son of a ship merchant. He became active in colonial opposition to the British and served (1774–1775) as a member of the Massachusetts Provincial Congress. He was a member (1776–1781) of the Second Continental Congress and was also a delegate (1782–1785) to the Congress of the Confederation. As a member (1789–1793) of the House of Representatives, Gerry frequently changed his position on matters of national policy. He sided with **Thomas Jefferson** (*see*) against the concept of a strong central government. At the same time, he mistrusted the common man and wished to protect "the commercial and monied interest." Sent by President **John Adams** (*see*) to obtain a treaty with France in 1797, Gerry became one of those involved in the notorious **XYZ Affair** (*see*). Ignoring his fellow diplomats, John Marshall (1755–1835) and **Charles Cotesworth Pinckney** (*see*), Gerry negotiated secretly with the French foreign minister, **Talleyrand** (*see*). He was recalled by Adams in 1798. Gerry was elected governor of Massachusetts in 1810, after four successive defeats. His political

Elbridge Gerry

technique of getting election districts rearranged to benefit his own party gave rise to the term *gerrymander*. Gerry was elected Vice-President when **James Madison** (*see*) was reelected President in 1812.

GHENT, Peace of. *See* **Peace of Ghent.**

H

HAMILTON, Alexander (1755–1804). As the first Secretary of the Treasury (1789–1795), Hamilton was very influential in shaping the American political and economic system. He was born on the island of Nevis, in the British West Indies. He received little formal schooling before entering King's College (now Columbia University) in New York in 1773. He wrote pamphlets critical of the British before the Revolution and took part in campaigns around New York after its outbreak. From 1777, he served as secretary and aide to **George Washington** (*see*) and fought at the Battle of Yorktown, Virginia, in 1781. His

marriage in 1780 to the daughter of General Philip Schuyler (1733–1804) brought him wealth and political influence. He served (1782–1783 and 1787–1788) in the Congress of the Confederation and opened a law office in New York City in 1783. Critical of the Articles of Confederation, under which the new Republic was governed, Hamilton argued for a stronger union and actively campaigned in 1787 for the new **Constitution** (*see*). Together with **James Madison** and **John Jay** (*see both*), Hamilton wrote most of the famous essays that make up *The Federalist Papers* (*see*), urging the ratification of the Constitution. Appointed Secretary of the Treasury in Washington's cabinet in 1789, Hamilton set about establishing a strong central government. Among his proposals were the assumption by the federal government of state debts, the levying of excise taxes, the establishment of a national bank, and federal support of agriculture. Almost all of Hamilton's program was passed by Congress, but not without bitter opposition from the followers of Madison and **Thomas**

Alexander Hamilton

Jefferson (*see*), who viewed strong federal power as a threat to the independence of the states. Industrial and commercial interests soon rallied to Hamilton's Federalist Party, while the advocates of states' rights formed the Democratic-Republican Party. Hamilton demonstrated his determination to impose federal authority throughout the nation by persuading Washington to use militia to crush the **Whiskey Rebellion** (*see*) in Pennsylvania in 1794. Hamilton resigned from the cabinet in 1795 to return to his law practice. As the Federalist Party leader in New York, he used his political influence to deny **Aaron Burr** (*see*) the Presidency in 1800 and the governorship of New York in 1804. That same year, Burr challenged him to a duel, which was fought at Weehawken, New Jersey, on July 11, 1804. Hamilton shot into the air, but Burr took aim and seriously wounded him. Hamilton died the following day.

HARTFORD CONVENTION.

From December 15, 1814, to January 5, 1815, 26 New Englanders met in secret sessions at Hartford, Connecticut, to discuss their opposition to government policies—especially the War of 1812. Eastern business interests particularly had suffered during the war because of the curtailment of foreign trade. Some of the delegates, all of whom were supporters of the Federalist Party, urged secession from the United States and a separate peace treaty with Britain. However, the convention was controlled by more cautious delegates, such as **Harrison Gray Otis** (*see*), who wanted their problems solved by constitutional changes. The convention adopted resolutions seeking, among other things, state authority to pro-

tect citizens from unconstitutional acts by the federal government, interstate cooperation in repelling enemy attacks, and constitutional amendments limiting the power of the government to restrict trade and declare war. The convention adjourned with plans to reconvene in June, 1815, but before then the war had officially ended. The Hartford Convention subsequently became an object of national scorn, and its members were accused of treason. As a result, the Federalist Party's influence rapidly declined.

HULL, Isaac (1773–1843). Hull commanded the famous *Constitution* (*see*) during her victory over the British frigate *Guerriere* in the first major sea battle of the War of 1812. Born in Massachusetts, Hull went to sea at 14 and two years later saved his captain's life in a shipwreck. He became a lieutenant in the United States Navy in 1798. During the Tripolitan War (*see* **Barbary Wars**), Hull, commanding his own ship, supported **William Eaton** (*see*) in the capture of Derna, Tripoli. In 1810, Hull was given command of the *Constitution*. When America declared war on England in 1812, Hull borrowed money to provision his ship and put to sea without orders. On August 19, he sighted the 38-gun British frigate *Guerriere* off the coast of Nova Scotia. Hull bore down on her—"rather too boldly for an American," the British captain said, as he tried unsuccessfully to maneuver away from his opponent's guns—and defeated her in a fierce 30-minute battle (*see pp. 320–321*). After his return to Boston, Hull was given command of the Boston Navy Yard. His victory, for which Congress awarded him a gold medal, had an important effect on the

nation's morale. He later served in squadrons patrolling the South American coast in 1824 and the Mediterranean in 1838. He retired in 1841.

HULL, William (1753–1825). A lawyer who had served as an officer in several major battles of the Revolution, Hull became governor of the Michigan Territory in 1805. At the outset of the War of 1812, he was put in command of American forces in the territory and crossed from Detroit into Canada with the intention of securing control of Lake Erie. Hull delayed launching his attack against the British, hoping that the Canadian militia would desert. In the meantime, his lines of communication were cut. Hull was finally forced to retreat to Detroit. There, on August 16, 1812, he surrendered his army of 2,000 men without a fight to the British general **Sir Isaac Brock** (*see*). Hull was subsequently court-martialed. He was found guilty of cowardice and neglect of duty and

William Hull

was sentenced to be shot. However, President **James Madison** (*see*) prevented the execution because of Hull's service in the Revolution. Instead, he was released from the army. Three days after Hull's unheroic surrender of Detroit, his nephew, **Isaac Hull** (*see*), commanded the *Constitution* in the nation's first major sea victory, defeating the British frigate *Guerriere* off the coast of Nova Scotia.

J

JACKSON, Andrew (1767–1845). Andrew Jackson, a rugged individualist who enjoyed gambling and racehorses, became a national hero at the Battle of **New Orleans** (*see*) in 1815. Born in the Waxhaw settlement in South Carolina, Jackson served in the American Revolution at the age of 13. He was captured by the British and was struck on the arm and head with a sword by an English officer whose boots he had refused to shine. Jackson became a lawyer in 1787. The following year, he settled in Nashville, then part of the western district of North Carolina. Jackson established a law practice there and was soon appointed prosecuting attorney general of the district. There he met Mrs. Rachel Donelson Robards (1767–1828), whom he married in 1791. Mrs. Robards believed she had been legally divorced by her first husband. Two years later, the Jacksons discovered that the divorce had not been valid at the time of their marriage, so they took new vows in 1794. The second ceremony did not end the scandalous rumors, which persisted throughout their lives. To defend Rachel's name, Jackson killed a man in a duel. In 1795, he

Andrew Jackson

bought a tract of land near Nashville, where he built The Hermitage, which became his home. When the western district was granted statehood as Tennessee in 1796, Jackson was elected a delegate to the state's constitutional convention. He tried unsuccessfully to eliminate the religious requirement for state office in Tennessee. Jackson served as Tennessee's first Congressman from December, 1796, to March, 1797. He then was a United States Senator for less than a year before returning in 1798 to Nashville, where he was appointed a judge of the Tennessee superior court. Although he retired in 1804, Jackson held the rank of major general in the state militia. When the War of 1812 broke out, he recruited 2,500 men and earned a reputation for sharing hardships with his soldiers, who nicknamed him Old Hickory. After the Creek Indians massacred the settlers at Fort Mims on the Alabama River on August 30, 1813, Tennessee was asked to send troops to subdue the Indians. Jackson was given command of the Tennessee forces, and on March 27, 1814, he defeated the Creeks at the Horseshoe Bend of the Tallapoosa River. This victory led to his appointment as a major general in the United States

Army. He was soon called upon to defend New Orleans from an impending British attack. Jackson's victory in the Battle of New Orleans on January 8, 1815 (*see p. 349 and back endsheet*), was the turning point in his career. The acclaim he won as the "Hero of New Orleans" helped him to become President in 1829. (*Entry continues in Volume 5.*)

JAY, John (1745–1829). The climax of Jay's long career of public service was his appointment in 1789 by **George Washington** (*see*) as the first Chief Justice of the United States. Jay was born in New York City, the son of a wealthy Dutch family. He graduated from King's College (now Columbia University) in 1764 and practiced law in New York between 1768 and 1776. Although active early in the patriot cause, Jay did not favor separation from England until this step became unavoidable. Jay was a member (1774–1779) of both the First and Second Continental Congresses and served as president of the latter (1778–1779). He was sent to Spain in 1779 to request aid for

NEW YORK PUBLIC LIBRARY

John Jay

E128

the Revolution but was unable to obtain any major assistance. Two years later, Jay, together with Benjamin Franklin (1706–1790) and **John Adams** (*see*), negotiated the Treaty of Paris, which officially ended the war with Britain. Jay was criticized at that time for ignoring America's ally, France, and for failing to obtain more concessions from the British, especially American control of Canada. Nevertheless, he was appointed secretary of foreign affairs by the Congress of the Confederation in 1784. A proponent of a stronger central government, Jay joined **James Madison** and **Alexander Hamilton** (*see both*) in writing *The Federalist Papers* (*see*), which urged the adoption of the **Constitution** (*see*). Chief Justice Jay was sent to London in 1794 by Washington to negotiate Anglo-American disputes. The resulting agreement with Britain, known as **Jay's Treaty** (*see*), aroused a storm of protest from rival Democratic-Republicans and the French, both of whom claimed that Jay had again conceded too much to England. Jay resigned from the Supreme Court in 1795 to become governor of New York, a post he held until 1801. He then retired to his farm in Westchester County.

JAY'S TREATY. Signed by the United States and Britain on November 19, 1794, this treaty was an attempt to settle disputes dating back to the Revolutionary War. In April, 1794, President **George Washington** (*see*), fearing another war with Britain, sent Chief Justice **John Jay** (*see*) to London to negotiate the grievances. Agreement was reached with the British foreign minister, William Wyndham Grenville (1759–1834), on the following points: (1) Northwest military posts occupied by the British would be evacuated by June, 1796; (2) boundary disputes and questions about prerevolutionary debts would be settled by joint commissions; (3) the British would have unrestricted access to American ports and the Mississippi River; and (4) American vessels would have free access to British ports, with the exception of those in the West Indies. However, the treaty ignored such important areas of friction as the British seizure of American ships and sailors and British-inspired Indian attacks on settlers in the West. **Alexander Hamilton** (*see*) and other Federalists defended Jay's Treaty by arguing that the concessions had to be made or Britain would cut off its trade with the United States. Without the custom duties collected on British goods, they argued, the American government would collapse. Jeffersonian Republicans denounced the treaty as a violation of American rights and commercial interests, as well as the American alliance of 1778 with France. After a heated debate, the Senate ratified a slightly amended form of Jay's Treaty on June 24, 1795. The unsettled disputes later led to the War of 1812.

JEFFERSON, Thomas (*Continued from Volume 3*). Jefferson came out of retirement in 1783 when he was elected to represent Virginia in the Congress of the Confederation (1781–1789). During his two-year term, he was responsible for, among other things, perfecting the decimal system of currency still in use and suggesting legislation for organizing the sparsely settled Northwest Territory. In 1785, Jefferson succeeded Benjamin Franklin (1706–1790) as minister to France. Although not present when the **Constitution** (*see*) was drawn up, he favored its ratification but strongly objected to the lack of a bill of rights. Jefferson, who witnessed the fall of the Bastille on July 14, 1789, at first supported the **French Revolution** (*see*) but later deplored the terror that dominated France. He returned to America in 1789 and became Secretary of State under **George Washington** (*see*). The disputes that subsequently developed between Jefferson and **Alexander Hamilton** (*see*), the Secretary of the Treasury, led to the formation of America's first political parties. The supporters of Jefferson, called Democratic-Republicans, opposed a strong central government and favored the development of an economy based on farming. They also favored an alliance with France. On the other hand, Hamilton's supporters, known as Federalists, were for a strong central government and advocated commercial and industrial expansion. They were pro-British. The modern Democratic Party traces its origin to Jefferson's Democratic-Republican Party. In 1793, Jefferson resigned his cabinet post because of strong differences with Hamilton's economic policies. He became Vice-President in 1797, serving under **John Adams** (*see*). He was first elected President in 1801 after he and **Aaron Burr** (*see*) received the same number of votes in the **electoral college** (*see*). The election was settled in the House of Representatives when Hamilton urged the Federalists to support Jefferson over Burr, whom he distrusted. The outstanding achievements in Jefferson's first administration (1801–1805) were the **Louisiana Purchase** (*see*) and the American victory in the Tripolitan War (*see* **Barbary**

Wars). Jefferson's second administration (1805–1809) was troubled by the British seizure of American ships and impressment of American seamen and by the resulting unpopular American embargo of British goods—issues that contributed to the War of 1812. Jefferson again retired in 1809 to his plantation, **Monticello** (*see*), in Virginia and 10 years later founded the University of Virginia at nearby Charlottesville. Jefferson, the author of the Declaration of Independence, died on July 4, 1826. No man in his time had been so deeply involved in so many aspects of human thought and endeavor (*see pp. 291–299*). His heirs followed the instructions he wrote for the epitaph on his tomb at Monticello:

aboard an American vessel anchored off that city. On the night of September 13–14, 1814, Key watched the British bombard Fort McHenry, near Baltimore, from the deck of his ship (*see p. 330–331*). He was inspired to compose his famous verses when he saw the American flag still flying over the fort the morning after the battle. Key later served as United States district attorney (1833–1841) for the District of Columbia.

KING, Rufus (1755–1827). An American diplomat and spokesman for the Federalist ideal of a strong central government, King fought briefly in the American Revolution. As a Massachusetts delegate (1784–1787) to the Congress of the Confederation, he

Rufus King

1825), he proposed plans for emancipating the slaves and re settling them in Africa. He made an unsuccessful bid for the Presidency in 1816. King was again appointed minister to Britain in 1825, but illness forced him to return to America the following year.

L

LAFFITE, Jean (1780?–1826?). Little is known of the early life of this French pirate who helped the Americans defeat the British at the Battle of **New Orleans** (*see*) in 1815. Laffite's band of privateers and smugglers operated from an island near New Orleans. They preyed on Spanish ships in the Gulf of Mexico and then sold their spoils at New Orleans, in violation of American revenue laws. The British told Laffite about their impending attack on the city and tried to enlist him on their side. The pirate chieftain, who was secretly loyal to the American cause, told the British that he would consider their offer of land and pardons for his men. Then he rushed to tell the Ameri-

'Here was buried
Thomas Jefferson
author of the Declaration of American Independance
of the Statute of Virginia for religious freedom
& Father of the University of Virginia.'

K

KEY, Francis Scott (1779–1843). Key wrote *The Star-Spangled Banner* (*see*), which became the national anthem of the United States. A native of Maryland, Key was an influential attorney in Washington, D.C., during the early 1800s. During the War of 1812, he was asked to obtain the release of an American who had been captured by the British. After successfully completing his mission, Key, expecting the British to attack Baltimore, remained

offered proposals that resulted in the prohibition of slavery in the Northwest Territory, which included lands north of the Ohio River. At the Constitutional Convention of 1787, King helped revise the **Constitution** (*see*) and was one of its signers. King later moved to New York and served as United States Senator from that state (1789–1796) and then as minister to Britain (1796–1803). He ran for Vice-President on the Federalist ticket in 1804 and again in 1808, but he was defeated both times. While serving again as Senator from New York (1813–

cans about the British plans. Despite a subsequent attack on his base by the American navy, Laffite and many of his men participated in the American victory at New Orleans on January 8, 1815. A month later, these pirates were pardoned for their past crimes by President **James Madison** (*see*). However, they soon returned to raiding shipping and coastal ports in the gulf. These raids occasionally brought them into conflict with the American authorities, but Laffite—known for his hospitality and gentlemanly manners, as well as his ruthlessness—was always able to settle matters with the government. His death was not recorded, but it was probably about 1826, at the time the pirates disappeared from the Caribbean.

LAWRENCE, James (1781–1813). An American naval hero of the early 1800s, Lawrence began his career as a midshipman in 1798. During the Tripolitan War (*see* **Barbary Wars**), he was second in command to **Stephen Decatur** (*see*) when Decatur engineered the sinking of the captured American frigate *Philadelphia* in the harbor of Tripoli. Lawrence later served as first lieutenant on the *Constitution* (*see*) and then commanded several ships, among them the *Hornet*. During the War of 1812, the *Hornet* sank the British brig of war *Peacock* in 1813 off British Guiana. Lawrence was hailed as a national hero for this victory. In the same year, he took command of the *Chesapeake* and fought a fierce but brief battle with the British frigate *Shannon* off Boston (*see pp. 326–327*). Before the *Chesapeake* was captured, Lawrence was mortally wounded. His dying words, "Don't give up the ship!" became a navy slogan.

John Ledyard

LEDYARD, John (1751–1789). This American adventurer ran away from missionary training at Dartmouth College and, as a corporal in the British marines, accompanied England's Captain James Cook (1728–1779) on his third and final voyage of exploration in the Pacific. The purpose of the voyage, begun in 1776, was to find a northwest passage around the North American continent. Although it failed to find the passage, the expedition discovered Hawaii and was the first British party to reach Nootka Sound and Alaska. Cook was killed by Hawaiian natives before the expedition returned to England in 1780. Ledyard, who refused to fight against his countrymen in the Revolution, spent the next two years confined to barracks. In 1782, he was assigned to a frigate patrolling American waters, where he jumped ship. After the war, Ledyard published his account of the Pacific voyage and tried to raise money for an expedition to cross the United States from west to east. Unable to do so, he went to France, where he met **Thomas**

Jefferson (*see*) and John Paul Jones (1747–1792). At first, both were enthusiastic about the project, and detailed plans were made. However, Jones finally decided that the expedition was too risky. Ledyard then resolved to walk alone across northern Europe and Asia in order to reach North America. He set out in 1786 from Hamburg, Germany, and reached Irkutsk in Siberia before he was arrested by the Russians, who rushed him back almost 4,000 miles and deposited him across the Polish border. Ledyard later received financial backing in England to explore the source of the Niger River in Africa. However, he died in Cairo before his expedition could be launched.

L'ENFANT, Pierre Charles (1754–1825). L'Enfant designed the city plan for **Washington, D.C.** (*see*). After studying architecture and engineering in his native Paris, L'Enfant came to America in 1777 to fight in the Revolution. He was promoted to the rank of major in May, 1783. Soon afterward, he designed the insignia for the Society of the Cincinnati, an organization of former officers of the Continental Army. In 1787, L'Enfant was chosen to remodel the old City Hall in New York into Federal Hall (*see p. 300*), which became the temporary headquarters of the United States government. The first Congress assembled there on March 4, 1789, and President **George Washington** (*see*) was inaugurated there on April 30, 1789. That same year, Washington asked L'Enfant to draw up plans for a new federal capital. In 1790, the President himself chose the site on the Potomac River for the permanent capital. By June, 1791, L'Enfant had finished his basic designs. The streets were to be constructed in a gridlike pattern, running from north to south and from east to west. In addition, wide avenues were to radiate from the principal points in the city, and central squares and attractive parks were to add a feeling of space. L'Enfant's unwillingness to compromise his plans and the unexpectedly high cost of the venture soon put him at odds with the federal authorities, including Washington, and L'Enfant was dismissed in February, 1792. He apparently was never fully paid for his work or for most of the other projects he undertook, and he died almost penniless. L'Enfant's plans for the capital were largely ignored until 1901, when their merits were recognized and his original design was readopted as the basis for all future development of the city.

LITTLE TURTLE (1752?–1812). Little Turtle, the chief of the Miami tribe, led an alliance of Indians to several victories against American settlers in the Ohio region of the Northwest Territory (*see* **Northwest Ordinance**) after the Revolution. A renowned orator and fighter, he went to war to prevent the further intrusion of white men on Indian lands. In 1790, Little Turtle defeated a band of Americans under Josiah Harmar (1753–1813), and the following year he successfully ambushed an army under General Arthur St. Clair (1736?–1818), killing or wounding 900 soldiers. Little Turtle commanded the attack on Fort Recovery in midsummer of 1794, suffering heavy losses. He subsequently advised the Indians to seek peace, but they ignored him. The Indians were then defeated on August 20, 1794, at the Battle of **Fallen Timbers** (*see*) by General Anthony

Wayne (1745–1796). In 1795, Little Turtle signed the Treaty of Greenville, in which the Indians gave up most of their land claims in Ohio. Thereafter, he aided the Americans and persuaded his tribesmen to yield their lands to them. It was due to his influence that the Miami tribe did not join the confederacy headed by the Shawnee chief, **Tecumseh** (*see*).

Little Turtle

LOUISIANA PURCHASE. The most important territorial acquisition of the United States was the vast, uncharted Louisiana Territory, purchased in 1803. By paying France $15,000,000 for the area, America doubled its size (*see p. 337*). The territory covered more than 800,000 square miles, stretching north from the mouth of the Mississippi River almost to Canada and as far west as the Rocky Mountains. It encompassed all or parts of 15 present-day states. Louisiana had been ceded by France to Spain in 1762, but by the secret Treaty of San Ildefonso in 1800, the territory was to be transferred back to France. Rumors about this treaty reached America when Spain began barring American traders

from the port of New Orleans in 1802, when the French were to assume control. The following year, President **Thomas Jefferson** sent **James Monroe** (*see both*) to France to aid the American minister, Robert R. Livingston (1746–1813), in negotiations to buy New Orleans and West Florida. Meanwhile, the French ruler, **Napoleon** (*see*), who once had had plans for an empire in North America, needed money to wage war on Britain. He had also become impatient at Spain's delay in transferring Louisiana to France. Napoleon decided to sell not only New Orleans but the rest of Louisiana as well. His surprise offer was immediately accepted, and the purchase agreement was signed on April 30, 1803. Later treaties with England and Spain settled the boundaries of the territory.

LOUIS PHILIPPE (1773–1850). The man who became the "Citizen King" of France (1830–1848) spent nearly four years in exile in the United States. During this time, he and his two brothers explored thousands of miles of the American frontier from Maine to New Orleans. Louis, a member of a noble family whose father was fifth in the line of succession to the throne of France, fled his nation in the middle of the **French Revolution** (*see*). He arrived in Philadelphia in October, 1796, and was soon joined by his younger brothers, whose release he had obtained from a French prison. In March, 1797, the three Frenchmen, dressed as ordinary citizens, set out to tour America. They visited Baltimore and Washington, D.C., and met **George Washington** (*see*) at Mount Vernon. Following a route that Washington traced on a map for them,

Louis Philippe

they journeyed through the Shenandoah Valley and Tennessee and Kentucky. The future king was not impressed with the Kentuckians he met. "They are the lowest sort of men I have ever seen," he wrote. "They are coarse, idle, and inhospitable to the utmost degree." After crossing Pennsylvania and western New York, the Frenchmen arrived in Philadelphia in July, having traveled about 2,000 miles. Before leaving the United States for England in 1800, Louis and his brothers also visited Boston and present-day Maine and sailed down the Mississippi River to New Orleans. Years later, as king of France, Louis said that his American adventures "have had a great influence on my political opinions and on my judgment of the course of human affairs." When a new revolution broke out in 1848, Louis and the queen were driven into exile in England.

M

MACLAY, William (1734–1804). Maclay, a Senator from Pennsylvania (1789–1791), kept a diary that is the only continuous account of the activities of the Senate's first session. This journal, first published in 1880, provides interesting sidelights into early disputes over the **Constitution** (*see*) and debt and tariff laws. Maclay was an opponent of the financial policies of **Alexander Hamilton** (*see*), the first Secretary of the Treasury, supporting instead the interests of small farmers who wanted a weak central government. Before becoming a Senator, Maclay had served in the French and Indian War (1754–1763) and had held various public offices in Pennsylvania.

MACON, Nathaniel (1758–1837). In 1810, as chairman of the House Committee on Foreign Relations, Macon presented two bills to the House that were named after him, Macon's Bill No. 1 and **Macon's Bill No. 2** (*see*). Actually, he wrote neither. After the first bill—designed to hamper British shipping—was defeated, he opposed the second when it was passed in May, 1810. Macon's Bill No. 2 authorized the President to establish exclusive trading privileges with either Britain or France, depending on which nation became the first to cease interfering with American commerce. Macon, who was born in North Carolina, fought in the Revolution and studied law before entering state politics in 1781. He was a member of Congress for 37 years, serving first in the House of Representatives (1791–1815) and then in the Senate (1815–1828). A champion of states' rights and personal liberty, Macon believed the Constitution gave too much power to the federal government. An unwavering advocate of slavery, Macon consistently opposed all liberal legislation introduced in Congress.

MACON'S BILL NO. 2. Named for the chairman of the House Committee on Foreign Affairs, **Nathaniel Macon** (*see*), this strange piece of legislation replaced the **Non-Intercourse Act** (*see*). The bill, which became law on May 1, 1810, allowed American ships to resume trade with all nations, including England and France, which were then at war. However, if either of the warring nations removed its anti-American trade restrictions within a year, the bill promised that a trade ban against the other nation would go into effect within three months. When President **James Madison** (*see*) interpreted an overture from France as an end to its restrictions on American trade, he ceased commerce with Britain. The British reacted by intensifying their impressment of American sailors and blockading New York. However, on June 16, 1812, the British decided to repeal their restrictions on American shipping. Unaware of this action, the United States declared war on Britain two days later.

MADISON, Dolley (1768–1849). The wife of the fourth President, Dolley was born in Guilford County, North Carolina. Her name at birth was Dorothea Payne. She grew up in Virginia and moved with her family to Philadelphia in 1783. Seven years later, she married John Todd, Jr., a Quaker lawyer. She bore him two sons, but the second one died, along with his father, in a yellow-fever epidemic of 1793. She did not remain a widow for very long. **Aaron Burr** (*see*) introduced her to **James Madison** (*see*), whom she married on September 15, 1794. When her husband became Secretary of State (1801–1809) in the administration of **Thomas Jeffer-**

Dolley Madison

son (*see*), Dolley functioned as the widowed President's official hostess at the White House. Her social graces proved invaluable to her husband's successful campaigns for the Presidency in 1808 and 1812. As the nation's first lady, she charmed the political and intellectual leaders of the young nation, including novelist Washington Irving (1783–1859), who remembered her as "a fine, portly, buxom dame." When the British set fire to the capital during the War of 1812, Dolley managed to save numerous state papers and an important portrait of George Washington before the White House was burned.

MADISON, James (1751–1836). Remembered as "the master-builder of the Constitution," Madison was the fourth President of the United States. He was born in Port Conway, Virginia, and graduated from the College of New Jersey (now Princeton University) in 1771. Madison served briefly (1780–1781) in the Second Continental Congress and then was a

member (1781–1783 and 1787–1788) of the Congress of the Confederation, in which he strove to strengthen the power of the national government. The notes he took at the Constitutional Convention of 1787 were published in 1840. They provide the chief record of the daily proceedings. Madison was instrumental in drafting the **Virginia Plan** (*see*), which, among other things, called for legislative, executive, and judicial branches in the new government and for the indirect election of a President by a group of electors. Much of this plan was adopted as the basis of the **Constitution** (*see*). After the adjournment of the convention, Madison, together with **John Jay** and **Alexander Hamilton** (*see both*), contributed to a series of essays called *The Federalist Papers* (*see*) to promote ratification of the Constitution. During the first session of the new Congress, Madison, a Representative (1789–1797), helped to draw up the first 10 amendments to the Constitution, known as the **Bill of Rights** (*see*). From the early 1790s, Madison was a leader of the Democratic-Republican Party, which opposed Hamilton and his Federalist policies. In 1798, he and **Thomas Jefferson** (*see*) protested against the Federalist-inspired **Naturalization and Alien Acts** and the **Sedition Act** (*see both*). Together they wrote the Kentucky and Virginia Resolves, which stated that the individual states had the right to declare acts of the federal government unconstitutional. When Jefferson was elected President in 1800, Madison became his Secretary of State (1801–1809). His wife, **Dolley Madison** (*see*), served as hostess for the widowed Jefferson at the White House. As Secretary of State, Madison tried to protect

American maritime interests during the war between England and France. He proposed a policy of "peaceful coercion," which resulted in the **Embargo Act** (*see*) in 1807 against the warring nations. Madison succeeded Jefferson to the Presidency in 1809. His administration was characterized by difficulties and tragedy. Yielding to the "war hawks" in Congress, Madison declared war on England on June 18, 1812, although the nation was unprepared for a major conflict. In New England, "Mr. Madison's War" was so unpopular that the **Hartford Convention** (*see*) was called in 1814, and the possibility of Northern secession was seriously considered. After the war, Madison spent the remainder of his term in office encouraging domestic industries by sponsoring America's first protective tariff law. He also rechartered the Bank of the United States. Madison retired to his Virginia estate, Montpelier, in

James Madison

1817 and fell into debt because of his lavish entertaining there. He died virtually penniless on June 28, 1836.

James Monroe

MONROE, James (1758–1831). In his annual message to Congress in 1823, the fifth President of the United States warned European powers that any future attempt to colonize or intervene in the affairs of nations in Latin America would be regarded as an act hostile toward the United States. This controversial principle of American foreign policy later became known as the Monroe Doctrine and was later invoked by the United States to justify the invasion of a number of Latin-American nations in the 20th century. Monroe was born in Westmoreland County, Virginia. He abandoned studies at the College of William and Mary in 1776 to serve in the Revolution and fought in campaigns around New York and at the Battles of Brandywine and Germantown in Pennsylvania. Between 1780 and 1783, Monroe studied law under **Thomas Jefferson** (*see*), whose political philosophy he was soon to champion. After serving (1783–1786) in the Congress of the Confederation (1781–1789), he practiced law in Fredericksburg. As a member of the Virginia convention in 1788, he opposed ratification of the **Constitution** (*see*) on the ground that it endangered states' rights. Monroe was elected to the United States Senate in 1790 and often assailed the Federalist policies of President **George Washington** (*see*) and his Secretary of the Treasury, **Alexander Hamilton** (*see*). With Jefferson and **James Madison** (*see*), he helped to form the Democratic-Republican Party. Monroe later served as minister to France (1794–1796) but was recalled because of bitter policy disputes with Washington over **Jay's Treaty** (*see*). After a term as governor of Virginia (1799–1802), he was appointed by President Jefferson to help negotiate the **Louisiana Purchase** (*see*) with France in 1803. He also took part in unsuccessful talks to arrange treaties with Spain and England. After being defeated for the Presidency in 1808, Monroe was elected governor of Virginia in 1811. However, he resigned to join Madison's cabinet as Secretary of State (1811–1817). Under Madison, he was also briefly Secretary of War (1814–1815). Monroe was elected President in 1816 and overwhelmingly returned to office in 1820. The period of his administrations is often called the Era of Good Feelings. Seeking to minimize party rivalry, Monroe chose both Federalists and Democratic-Republicans to serve in his cabinet. During his Presidency, boundary disputes with Canada were settled, Florida was obtained from Spain in 1819, and the famous Monroe Doctrine was formulated. After leaving office in 1825, Monroe presided at the Virginia constitutional convention (1829–1830). He died on July 4, 1831.

MONTICELLO. Monticello, which means "little mountain" in Italian, was the estate designed and built by **Thomas Jefferson** (*see*) near Charlottesville, Virginia (*see pp. 298–299*). Jefferson began preparations for construction in 1767 and in November, 1770, moved into the first completed structure, a one-room brick out-

The mansion at Monticello appears on the back of the Jefferson nickel.

building. All the materials used in the construction of Monticello were produced on the estate. In 1770, Jefferson began building the main house, which was extensively remodeled in 1796. Monticello is one of the earliest examples of the architecture of the American classical revival. The mansion, which is built in the style of an Italian villa, has a Greek portico and a Roman dome as well as many colonial features. After Jefferson's death in 1826, its ownership passed through many hands until 1923, when it was purchased by the Thomas Jefferson Memorial Foundation. In 1954, after extensive restorations, Monticello was opened to the public.

MORRIS, Gouverneur (1752–1816). Morris was a Federalist statesman who actively supported a strong central government at the Constitutional Convention of 1787. Born into an aristocratic New York family, Morris entered politics as a delegate (1775–1777) to New York's Provincial Congress. He then represented New York at the Second Continental Congress before moving to Pennsylvania in 1779. In 1780, Morris wrote a brilliant series of essays on the American financial situation. These led to his appointment the following year as assistant to the federal superintendent of finance, Robert Morris (1734–1806), who was no relation. In this position, he devised a plan for a decimal system of coinage and suggested the word *cent*. At the Constitutional Convention of 1787, Morris was responsible for giving the **Constitution** (*see*) its final literary style. Morris went to France on business in 1789 and while there was appointed the American minister in 1792. He served for two years and returned

to America in 1798. He later was a Senator from New York (1800–1803) and chairman of the Erie Canal Commission (1810–1813).

MOUNT VERNON. George Washington (*see*) lived and died at Mount Vernon, his estate on the Potomac River in Fairfax County, Virginia. The property was acquired by the Washington family in 1690, and George's elder half brother, Lawrence Washington (1718–1752), built the central part of the main house in 1743. George became a frequent visitor to the house after 1748 and inherited it in 1761. Washington began enlarging the house in 1774, but the additions were not completed until after the Revolution. The mansion is a three-storied white clapboard structure (*see pp. 278–279*). It has a deep portico supported by columns and is surrounded by lawns, gardens, and a number of smaller buildings that once housed cooking, storage, and other quarters. The Mount Vernon Ladies' Association bought the estate from Washington's heirs shortly before the Civil War. Since then, it has been restored with much of Washington's own furniture or duplicate pieces made in his day. Mount Vernon, one of the best-preserved examples of an 18th-century Southern plantation, is now open to the public.

N

NAPOLEON BONAPARTE (1769–1821). Soon after coming to power in France, Napoleon, through his foreign minister, **Talleyrand** (*see*), negotiated the **Convention of 1800** (*see*). This treaty ended the undeclared naval hostilities between the United States and France that had been going

Napoleon Bonaparte

on for two years. Three years later, in need of gold to conduct a war with Britain and fearing that French possessions in North America would be impossible to defend, he sold the vast Louisiana Territory to the United States for $15,000,000 (*see* **Louisiana Purchase**). Napoleon's opposition to American trade with England, however, resulted in the French seizure of many American vessels. In addition, his diplomatic trickery helped to worsen relations between the United States and Britain (*see p. 344*) and bring on the War of 1812. Born Napoleone Buonaparte on the island of Corsica, he entered military school in France at the age of nine. He was commissioned a second lieutenant in the artillery in 1785 and soon allied himself with the leaders of the **French Revolution** (*see*). Shrewd, ambitious, and ruthless, Napoleon was a brigadier general by 1794 and commander of the army of Italy two years later. Victories in Italy, Austria, and Egypt advanced his reputation for military genius. After the ruling French Directory was overthrown in November, 1799, Napoleon was named first consul of France. He soon assumed absolute control of his nation, finally crowning himself as Emperor Napoleon I on December 2, 1804. Determined to establish French control over all Europe, Napoleon embarked on a series of wars known as the Napoleonic Wars. By 1810, France controlled seven kingdoms and 30 principalities. Napoleon's downfall began with his invasion of Russia in the summer of 1812. Less than 10% of his huge *Grande Armee* survived the devastating retreat from Moscow that winter. Paris fell to the combined force of his European enemies in 1814, and Napoleon was exiled to the Mediterranean island of Elba. He escaped in 1815 and attempted to regain power but was crushed by the British and Prussians at the Battle of Waterloo, in Belgium, on June 18, 1815. Napoleon died in exile on the island of St. Helena, off southwestern Africa.

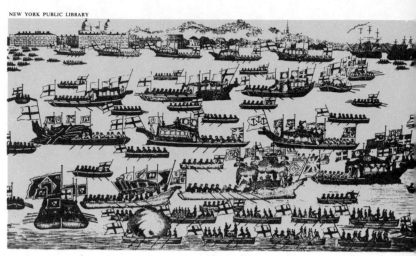

This engraving depicts Nelson's funeral procession on the Thames River.

NATURALIZATION and ALIEN ACTS. Like the **Sedition Act** (*see*), the Naturalization and Alien Acts were designed to weaken the power of the growing Democratic-Republican Party led by **Thomas Jefferson** (*see*). On June 18, 1798, the Federalist-controlled Congress passed the Naturalization Act, which extended from five years to 14 years the period of time an immigrant had to reside in the United States before qualifying for citizenship. The act was intended to limit the voting strength of the Democratic-Republicans, many of whom were recent immigrants. The Alien Act, which was passed on June 25, 1798, gave the Presi-

dent the power to imprison or deport anyone who was not a citizen and whom he regarded as dangerous to the peace and safety of the United States. At this time, a large number of immigrants from France, not yet naturalized as citizens, were residing in America. The pro-British Federalists, eager to get rid of these allies of the Democratic-Republicans, claimed that the "aliens" represented a threat to the United States. President **John Adams** (*see*), although a Federalist, refused to enforce the Alien Act, which expired in 1800. The Naturalization Act was repealed in 1802 during the administration of President Jefferson.

NELSON, Horatio (1758–1805). Viscount Nelson, one of England's greatest admirals, was given command of the British Mediterranean fleet in 1803 at the outbreak of the Napoleonic Wars between France and Britain and their allies. At the Battle of Trafalgar, fought near the Strait of Gibraltar on October 21, 1805, Nelson defeated a combined French and Spanish fleet. The victory cost

him his life but ended French naval dominance in Europe. **Napoleon** (*see*) then decided that the only way he could defeat the British was through economic warfare. Britain responded by taking measures that were among the primary causes of the War of 1812. These included interference with American shipping and the impressment of American seamen.

NEW JERSEY PLAN. The New Jersey Plan was put before the Constitutional Convention in mid-June, 1787, by **William Paterson** (*see*) as an alternative to the **Virginia Plan** (*see*). The main difference between the two plans concerned the character of the legislative branch of the federal government. The Virginia Plan favored the larger states by proposing a two-chamber legislature with representation according to population. The New Jersey proposal protected the interests of the smaller states by suggesting a one-chamber legislature in which each state would have equal representation. It also provided for an executive branch composed of more than one person and without veto power. By the **Connecticut Compromise** (*see*) of July 16, 1787, the convention agreed to create a two-chamber Congress in which the states would have equal representation in the Senate and representation according to population in the House.

NEW ORLEANS, Battle of. The Battle of New Orleans, which was fought on January 8, 1815, took place two weeks after the signing of the **Peace of Ghent** (*see*), which ended the War of 1812. In the autumn of 1814, while diplomats were negotiating peace terms in Europe, the British army was preparing its greatest undertaking of the war. Its aim was to occupy New Orleans and as much territory along the Gulf of Mexico as possible. The British intended to use their conquests as bargaining power in the peace talks. **Andrew Jackson** (*see*), the commander of American troops in the southwestern area, arrived in New Orleans on December 1, 1814, and set about strengthening the city's defenses. After several skirmishes between British and American troops in the area, the British commander, **Edward Pakenham** (*see*), decided to attack New Orleans on January 8, 1815 (*see p. 349 and back endsheet*). In less than half an hour, the Americans were able to inflict a decisive defeat on the British. The Americans suffered 71 casualties, of whom 13 were killed, while the British losses numbered more than 2,000 killed and wounded.

NON-IMPORTATION ACT. This was the first of four major acts passed by Congress in the first decade of the 19th century to protect American neutrality on the seas during the Napoleonic Wars (*see* **Napoleon**). From the start of hostilities between Britain and France in 1803, British ships were almost exclusively committed to military uses. The United States profited from this by expanding its merchant marine and becoming the chief neutral trading nation. To hinder American commerce with France, Britain began seizing American ships about 1805 and impressing American sailors into the British navy. Congress, on April 18, 1806, retaliated by passing the Non-Importation Act. It prohibited the importation of certain British goods into the United States. At the same time, a diplomatic mission was sent to England to negotiate an end to the seizures and impressments. However, the mission failed to get Britain to change her policy. The Non-Importation Act was suspended on December 19, 1806. It was replaced the following year by the more effective **Embargo Act** (*see*).

NON-INTERCOURSE ACT. Passed by Congress on March 1, 1809, the Non-Intercourse Act was a weak version of the **Embargo Act** (*see*), which it replaced. The new law was also part of an effort by the United States in the early 1800s to end European interference with American shipping. The Embargo Act had nearly ruined American commerce by prohibiting almost all foreign trade. By contrast, the Non-Intercourse Act reopened trade with all nations except warring Britain and France and their territories. It also promised to restore relations with the first of these two nations to recognize America's rights of neutrality. **Macon's Bill No. 2** (*see*) was substituted for the act when it expired in 1810.

NORTHWEST ORDINANCE. Also known as the Ordinance of 1787, the Northwest Ordinance was enacted by the Congress of the Confederation on July 13, 1787. The ordinance established the pattern for the development of the West along lines basic to American democracy (*see p. 285*). The ordinance created the Northwest Territory, which included all lands northwest of the Ohio River between the Great Lakes and the Mississippi River. It also established a procedure for the territory's admission to the Union as separate states. At first, the entire territory was to be governed by a congressionally appointed commission. As soon as there were 5,000 free adult males in the territory, it could elect a legislature and send a nonvoting representative to Congress. When any part of the territory had a voting population of 60,000, it could apply for statehood. The ordinance decreed that between three and five states could be formed from the Northwest Territory. These were to be "on an equal footing with the original states in all respects whatever." The ordinance also contained a bill of rights that established freedom of worship and trial by jury in the territory, prohibited slavery and primogeniture, and encouraged education. The five states that were created from the territory, all in the first half of the 19th century, were Ohio, Indiana, Illinois, Michigan, and Wisconsin.

O

ORDINANCE OF 1785. The Ordinance of 1785, which was enacted by the Congress of the Confederation on May 20, 1785, is considered one of the most important legislative acts in American history. It established a method

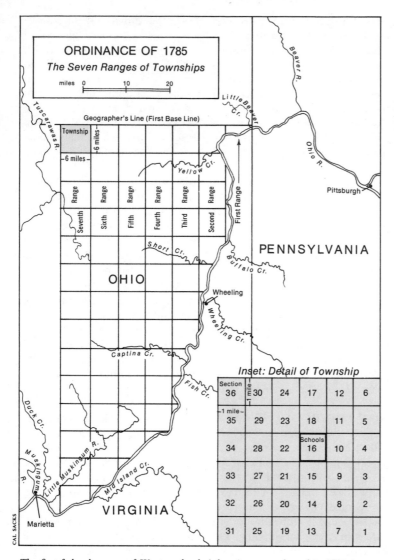

ORDINANCE OF 1785
The Seven Ranges of Townships

miles 0 — 10 — 20

Geographer's Line (First Base Line)

Township — 6 miles — 6 miles

Range Seventh / Range Sixth / Range Fifth / Range Fourth / Range Third / Range Second / First Range

Tuscarawas R.

Little Beaver Cr.

Beaver R.

Yellow Cr.

Ohio R.

Pittsburgh

Short Cr.

Buffalo Cr.

PENNSYLVANIA

OHIO

Wheeling

Wheeling Cr.

Captina Cr.

Fish Cr.

Duck Cr.

Muskingum R.

Little Muskingum R.

Mid Island Cr.

VIRGINIA

Marietta

CAL SACKS

Inset: Detail of Township

Section 36	30	24	17	12	6
35	29	23	18	11	5
34	28	22	Schools 16	10	4
33	27	21	15	9	3
32	26	20	14	8	2
31	25	19	13	7	1

(1 mile markings on inset)

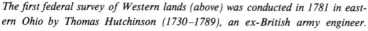

The first federal survey of Western lands (above) was conducted in 1781 in eastern Ohio by Thomas Hutchinson (1730–1789), an ex-British army engineer.

for the survey and sale of Western lands by the federal government. In 1780, the original 13 states began to cede their claims to land between the Appalachian Mountains and the Mississippi River. At the same time, a bitter debate developed over how to dispose of these lands once they were acquired by the federal government. Some people believed that the lands should be surveyed into

uniform units before sale, while others thought that individual pioneers should be able to make their claims as they saw fit. The Ordinance of 1785 was a compromise solution. It decreed that the federal government would survey the lands into individual townships, each of which was to be six miles square. These townships were to be subdivided into 36 lots of 640 acres (one square mile)

each. These lots could then be divided into rectangular units. Once this had been completed, the townships were to be sold at public auction for not less than $1 an acre. The ordinance also contained a provision setting aside one lot in each township to provide funds to maintain public schools. As the United States acquired further territory—as in the case of the **Louisiana Purchase** (*see*) in 1803 —the ordinance was applied to these new lands, until eventually its jurisdiction stretched to the Pacific Ocean.

OSGOOD, Samuel (1748–1813). A soldier and legislator, Osgood became a captain of a company of Minutemen at the outbreak of the Revolution. Elevated to major, he served as aide to General Artemas Ward (1727–1800) and was later promoted to colonel. Among other positions he held, Osgood served in the Massachusetts constitutional convention of 1779, the state senate in 1780, and the Congress of the Confederation from 1781 to 1784. In Congress, Osgood was especially active in preparing legislation related to business and finance. He opposed ratification of the **Constitution** (*see*) because he believed it gave too much power to the federal government. In 1785, Osgood was chosen as one of three commissioners of the Treasury, and four years afterward he was appointed Postmaster General. He was elected to the New York Assembly in 1800.

OTIS, Harrison Gray (1765– 1848). The nephew of patriot James Otis (1725–1783), Otis was chiefly responsible for summoning the **Hartford Convention** (*see*) in 1814. He hoped the convention would provide a public platform for those New Englanders who were dissatisfied with the federal government because of the War of 1812. Otis headed a delegation chosen by the convention to present a list of grievances to the federal government. Before he could do so, the war ended, and the convention became the butt of national ridicule. Otis was later a United States Senator (1817–1822) and mayor of Boston (1829–1832).

P

PAKENHAM, Sir Edward Michael (1778–1815) Pakenham, a major general, commanded the British army at the Battle of **New Orleans** (*see*) in 1815. He entered the British army at the age of 16 and was commissioned a colonel seven months later. Pakenham fought valiantly in Europe during the Napoleonic Wars and was promoted to major general in 1812. In November, 1814, he sailed from Jamaica with a force of 7,500 soldiers to capture New Orleans. After several preliminary skirmishes, he launched his main attack on the city on January 8, 1815 (*see back endsheet*). Pakenham was killed while trying to rally his men (*see p. 349*).

PATERSON, WILLIAM (1745–1806). Paterson proposed the **New Jersey Plan** (*see*), which favored the smaller states, at the Constitutional Convention of 1787. After graduation from the College of New Jersey (now Princeton University) in 1763, Paterson studied law. He served as attorney general of New Jersey (1776–1783) before he was chosen to represent his state at the Constitutional Convention. Paterson was a signer of the United States Constitution.

He later served as a Senator from New Jersey (1789–1790), as governor of his state (1790–1793), and as an Associate Justice of the United States Supreme Court (1793–1806).

PEACE OF GHENT. The Peace of Ghent, which was signed on December 24, 1814, officially ended the War of 1812. Even before the war against England had been declared, American diplomats were preparing to start peace negotiations. In preliminary meetings with British officials, they demanded a stop to the impressment of American sailors and respect for the neutral rights of the nation. However, by June, 1814, the military situation was so gloomy that the Americans dropped virtually all their demands. The British, too, were weary of an expensive and indecisive war and suggested a peace conference at the Belgian town of Ghent. Talks began in the summer of 1814, and a treaty was signed the following Christmas Eve. Although the original American demands were not mentioned, the Peace of Ghent ended hostilities and restored the boundaries that had been agreed upon in the Treaty of Paris, which settled the American Revolution. News of the peace did not reach America until February 11, 1815, a month after the Battle of **New Orleans** (*see*) was fought.

PEALE, Charles Willson (1741–1827). A man of varied interests and talents (*see pp. 350–358*), Peale was recognized as a leading portrait artist of his time. Born in Maryland, Peale dabbled in different trades and then studied painting in Boston in 1765 under John Singleton Copley (1738–1815) and in London for three years at the

Charles Willson Peale

studio of American-born Benjamin West (1730–1813). On his return to America, he painted likenesses of many prominent Americans, but he is probably best remembered for his 60 realistic portraits of **George Washington** (*see*), who posed for him on seven occasions. In 1776, Peale moved to Philadelphia and joined the city's militia. He saw action at the Battles of Trenton and Princeton in the winter of 1776–1777. After the war, Peale exhibited portraits he had painted of revolutionary officers in a picture gallery in back of his house. An avid naturalist, he also displayed there scientific curiosities, stuffed animals, and prehistoric relics. In 1794, his collection of 100,000 items was housed in the hall of the **American Philosophical Society** (*see*). Peale obtained in 1801 the rights to a mastodon skeleton discovered on a New York farm, and he persuaded the society to finance the excavation (*see p. 297*). In 1802, Peale moved his museum to Independence Hall, and the collection subsequently was incorporated as the Philadelphia Museum. Three years later, he helped to establish the Pennsylvania Academy of Fine Arts, the nation's first public art gallery.

PERRY, Oliver Hazard (1785–1819). The hero of the Battle of Lake Erie, Perry entered the navy as a midshipman when he was 14. He served in the West Indies and the Mediterranean. Perry received his first command, the *Revenge*, in 1809. She ran aground in a fog off Rhode Island two years later and sank, but a court of inquiry acquitted Perry of any blame for her loss. At the outbreak of the War of 1812, Perry, then commanding a division of gunboats at Newport, requested duty on the Great Lakes under Commodore Isaac Chauncey (1772–1840). In 1813, he was sent to Erie, Pennsylvania, to build and equip a fleet in order to challenge British control of Lake Erie. On September 10, 1813, he defeated and captured the British fleet (*see pp. 328–329*). During the battle, Perry's flagship, the *Lawrence,* was badly damaged, but Perry rowed to the *Niagara* and continued fighting. This victory marked the first time an entire British fleet was forced to surrender. Perry was subsequently promoted to captain. In 1819, while on a mission to South America, he contracted yellow fever in Venezuela and died. His brother, Matthew C. Perry (1794–1858), also a naval officer, established diplomatic and trade relations with Japan.

PICKERING, Timothy (1745–1829). Pickering, a Secretary of State who favored the British, was dismissed from office by President **John Adams** (*see*) in 1800 for trying to get America to declare war on France. In doing so, Pickering was undermining the President's efforts to end two years of naval hostilities with France through diplomacy (*see* **Convention of 1800**). Born in Salem, Massachusetts, Pickering had fought in several Revolutionary War battles and served as adjutant general of the Continental Army (1777–1778), on the Board of War (1777–1780), and as quartermaster general (1780–1783). In 1785, he moved to Pennsylvania and was a delegate to the state constitutional convention (1789–1790). He then served as Postmaster General (1791–1795), Secretary of War (1795), and Secretary of State (1795–1800). After his dismissal from the cabinet, Pickering returned to Massachusetts. He retained his bitterly anti-French attitudes while serving in Congress, first as a Senator (1803–1811) and later as a Representative (1813–1817). Pickering went so far as to contemplate the formation of a separate confederation of Northern states, and he firmly opposed the War of 1812 against England.

PINCKNEY, Charles Cotesworth (1746–1825). Together with **Elbridge Gerry** (*see*) and John Marshall (1755–1835), Pinckney was appointed in 1796 by President **John Adams** (*see*) to negotiate a treaty with France. In the resulting **XYZ Affair** (*see*), agents of the French foreign minister, **Talleyrand** (*see*), demanded a bribe as the price of peace. Pinckney's reply—"No, no, not a sixpence!"— gave rise to the familiar expression, "Millions for defense, but not one cent for tribute." Pinckney, a native of Charleston, South Carolina, studied at Oxford University in England and later practiced law in Charleston. During the Revolution, he was an aide to **George Washington** (*see*) at the Battles of Brandywine and Germantown and also served in the South Carolina legislature. He was captured when the British seized Charleston in 1780 but was released two years later. A delegate to the Constitutional Convention in 1787, he helped draft the **Constitution** (*see*). He declined repeated offers from Washington to serve in his cabinet but in 1796 agreed to be American minister to France, although the French never accepted his diplomatic credentials. Pinckney was the unsuccessful Federalist nominee for Vice-President in the election of 1800 and for President in 1804 and 1808.

PREBLE, Edward (1761–1807). As commander of a Mediterranean squadron during the Tripolitan War (*see* **Barbary Wars**), Preble helped train some of the most famous naval officers of the War of 1812, including **Stephen Decatur, William Bainbridge,** and **Isaac Hull** (*see all*). Preble was a midshipman in the Massachusetts navy during the Revolution and afterward served in the merchant

Edward Preble

marine. When undeclared naval hostilities with France began in 1798, Preble entered the newly formed United States Navy as a lieutenant. For the next two years he served in the West Indies and East Indies, where he helped protect American commerce from French privateers. He was promoted to captain in May, 1799. In the late summer of 1804, during the Tripolitan War, Preble's squadron blockaded Tripoli and attacked the heavily fortified port five times, but was unable to capture it. Relieved of his command, Preble returned to the United States and built gunboats for the navy until his death.

PREVOST, Sir George (1767–1816). Prevost, the governor-general of Canada (1811–1815), was commander in chief of all British forces in that region during the War of 1812. His defeat at the Battle of Plattsburg, New York, in 1814 hastened the war's end. Earlier, Prevost had been forced to make a humiliating retreat following the Battle of Sackets Harbor on Lake Ontario in late May, 1813. In September of the following year, he commanded a combined land and water campaign along the western shore of Lake Champlain. On September 11, at Plattsburg, Prevost failed to provide adequate ground support for his naval force in Lake Champlain. The British were decisively routed in both the land and naval battles and were forced to retreat into Canada. Prevost was subsequently relieved of his command.

R

RANDOLPH, Edmund (1753–1813). Randolph proposed the **Virginia Plan** (*see*), which favored

the more populated states, during the Constitutional Convention in 1787. Born in Williamsburg, Randolph, a lawyer, served as attorney general of Virginia (1776–1786), as a delegate (1779–1781) to the Second Continental Congress, and later was governor of Virginia (1786–1788). Although many features of the Virginia Plan were included in the **Constitution** (*see*), Randolph refused to sign the finished document on the ground that too much power was concentrated in the office of the President. However, he supported its ratification by Virginia because he believed the issue was "Union or no Union." Randolph served as the first Attorney General of the United States (1789–1794) before succeeding **Thomas Jefferson** (*see*) as Secretary of State. He played a prominent part in the negotiations connected with the controversial **Jay's Treaty** (*see*) with Britain in 1794. In August, 1795, Randolph was forced to resign because of accusations—later proved false—that he would welcome a bribe from the French government. He then practiced law and in 1807 was senior counsel to **Aaron Burr** (*see*) when the former Vice-President was tried for treason and subsequently acquitted by the Supreme Court on a legal technicality.

RITTENHOUSE, David (1732–1796). One of the foremost scientists of his day, Rittenhouse contributed to the fields of instrument making, astronomy, and mathematics. Born near Germantown, Pennsylvania, Rittenhouse was a self-taught scientist. At the age of 19, he opened an instrument and clock-making shop. In 1763, using devices made in his shop, Rittenhouse surveyed the Pennsylvania border in a boundary dis-

David Rittenhouse

pute with Maryland. His measurements were so accurate that he was subsequently commissioned to survey the borders of many other colonies. Rittenhouse constructed the first of two working models of the solar system (called "orreries") in 1767. The following year, he built an observatory in Philadelphia—with what was probably the first telescope made in America—to watch the planet Venus pass across the sun. During the Revolution, Rittenhouse served in the Pennsylvania Assembly and was president of the Council of Safety. He was treasurer of Pennsylvania from 1777 to 1789 and became the first director of the United States Mint in 1792. He succeeded Benjamin Franklin (1706–1790) as president of the **American Philosophical Society** (*see*) in 1791 and was reelected to the post every year until his death.

ROSS, Robert (1766–1814). Ross was the British general who captured and burned Washington, D.C., during the War of 1812. A veteran of the Napoleonic Wars, he was sent to America in 1814 with a 4,000-man army. His assignment was to create a "diversion" while British forces attacked the United States from Canada. Ross landed in Maryland in mid-August and headed toward the capital. The way was blocked by American forces under **William Winder** (*see*), but Ross easily routed them at the Battle of Bladensburg on August 24, 1814. By the following morning, Washington was in the hands of the British, and Ross ordered the burning of the city's major buildings. Encouraged by his victory, Ross then set out to capture Baltimore. His army landed at North Point, 14 miles from Baltimore, on September 12 and engaged an American army led by General John Stricker (1759–1825). The Americans retreated but the British suffered heavy losses, and Ross himself was killed in the fighting. The British withdrew their forces from Maryland after their fleet unsuccessfully shelled Fort McHenry outside Baltimore on September 13–14. The bombardment inspired **Francis Scott Key** to write *The Star-Spangled Banner* (*see both*).

RUTLEDGE, John (1739–1800). Rutledge succeeded **John Jay** (*see*) as Chief Justice of the Supreme Court in 1795 and served for six months before his nomination was rejected by the Senate. A South Carolina lawyer, Rutledge had served during the Revolution as president of the South Carolina General Assembly and as commander in chief of its militia when the British first threatened Charleston in 1776. He was elected governor in 1779 and combined forces with General Nathanael Greene (1742–1786) after Charleston finally fell to the British the next year. Rutledge resumed his duties as governor when the city was recaptured and was a member

of the Constitutional Convention in 1787. Rutledge was an Associate Justice of the Supreme Court from 1789 to 1791. Four years later, President **George Washington** (*see*) named him Chief Justice of the Supreme Court. However, Rutledge's bitter opposition to **Jay's Treaty** (*see*) eventually caused the Senate to reject his nomination. Because Rutledge was not confirmed, **Oliver Ellsworth** (*see*), his successor, is usually listed as the second Chief Justice.

S

SEDITION ACT. Passed by Congress on July 14, 1798, the Sedition Act made it a crime to "impede the operation of any law" or to take part in "any insurrection, riot, unlawful assembly, or combination." In addition, it imposed heavy penalties for criticizing the President or Congress in a "false, scandalous and malicious" way. This part of the act was an attempt to silence criticism of both the Federalist-controlled Congress and the administration of President **John Adams** (*see*). A number of prominent editors and printers —all rival Democratic-Republicans—were prosecuted under the Sedition Act, fined, and sent to prison. Like the **Naturalization and Alien Acts** (*see*), this legislation was a blatant political maneuver. It was widely attacked as a violation of the First Amendment to the Constitution (*see* **Bill of Rights**), which guarantees the freedom of speech and of the press. In opposing the Sedition Act, **James Madison** (*see*) argued that government officials were the servants, not the masters, of the people. The act aroused much popular resentment against the Federalist Party of **George Wash-**

ington and **Alexander Hamilton** (*see both*) and helped bring about its defeat in the election of 1800. The act expired on March 3, 1801, and was not renewed. President **Thomas Jefferson** (*see*) then pardoned those who had been imprisoned under it.

SHAYS' REBELLION. This uprising, named for one of its leaders, Daniel Shays (1747?–1825), involved debt-ridden farmers in western and central Massachusetts. Faced with high taxes, many of them were threatened with loss of their properties or imprisonment. The uprising lasted from August, 1786, to February, 1787. Groups of discontented farmers first met at county conventions and petitioned the state for rights they believed they had won in the Revolution. Among other things, they demanded court reforms and the issuance of paper money for paying their debts. After the Massachusetts legislature refused their demands, a band of armed farmers went to Northampton on August 29, 1786, and closed a court that was going to prosecute debtors. In September, about 500 insurgents, headed by Shays, a Revolutionary War veteran and local officeholder, stormed the town of Springfield to prevent the state supreme court from charging them with treason. Shays' soldiers were opposed by an equal number of militiamen, but bloodshed was avoided and both groups dispersed. Still dissatisfied, Shays led 1,200 men, armed mainly with pitchforks and staves, in an attack on the Springfield arsenal on January 25, 1787, but was repulsed. Three rebels were shot, and the rest fled. General Benjamin Lincoln (1733–1810) was placed in command of about 4,400 state troops, who rounded up the rebels. Most of them were pardoned. Shays escaped to Vermont but was later caught and sentenced to die. He was pardoned in 1788. Many of the farmers' demands were later granted by the legislature.

SHERMAN, Roger (1721–1793). Sherman sponsored the **Connecticut Compromise** (*see*) at the Constitutional Convention in 1787. The son of a Massachusetts farmer, Sherman became a lawyer in 1754. He helped draft the Declaration of Independence in 1776 and served in the Second Continental Congress (1775–1781) during the Revolution. In 1784, he was elected the first mayor of New Haven, Connecticut. Three years later, in order to form a stronger central government, he presented the Connecticut Compromise and successfully fought for its adoption. In 1789, Sherman was elected to the House, and two years later to the Senate, an office he held until his death.

STAR-SPANGLED BANNER, THE. This poem was enthusiastically received by the American public immediately after it was published in 1814. Although both the army and the navy regarded it for many years as the United States anthem, it did not officially become the national anthem until 1931, when Congress confirmed an Executive order of 1916 signed by President Woodrow Wilson (1856–1924). The poem was written by **Francis Scott Key** (*see*), who on the night of September 13–14, 1814, watched the British bombard Fort McHenry, near Baltimore. The next morning, he saw the American flag still flying over the fort and realized that the attack had failed. Inspired, he composed a poem, which was first printed in Baltimore under the title *The Defense of Fort McHenry.* This was changed to *The Star-Spangled Banner* in October, 1814. It is sung to a tune entitled *To Anacreon in Heaven,* a well-known English drinking song of the period.

STUART, Gilbert (1755–1828). Remembered chiefly for his paintings of **George Washington** (*see*), Stuart gained a reputation in American portraiture that remains unsurpassed. A native of Rhode Island, he went to England in 1775 and the following year became the pupil of American-born Benjamin West (1730–1813). Stuart set up his own studio in 1782, following a successful exhibition at the Royal Academy. Despite many commissions from leading personalities, including the royal family, Stuart fell into debt and fled to Ireland in 1787. He returned impoverished to America about 1792, hoping to become rich by painting portraits of Washington. Stuart established his studio in 1794 in Philadelphia. President Washington posed for three portraits, from which Stuart made dozens of

Gilbert Stuart's self-portrait

replicas. The so-called Athenaeum portrait of 1796 was later used on United States postage stamps. Unlike **Charles Willson Peale** (*see*), who painted realistically, Stuart idealized Washington's physical features, ignoring the changes in the aging President's appearance. Before moving to Boston in 1805, Stuart also painted **Thomas Jefferson, James Madison,** and **James Monroe** (*see all*). Stuart became increasingly eccentric as he grew older. He refused to paint people with dull faces, and he turned down many commissions. Often, he left paintings unfinished. He died virtually penniless.

T

TALLEYRAND, Charles Maurice de (1754–1838). As French foreign minister, Talleyrand was responsible in 1797 for the notorious **XYZ Affair** (*see*), which damaged relations between France and the United States and led to an undeclared naval war. Alarmed that outright war might be declared, he joined with President **John Adams** (*see*) in bringing about the **Convention of 1800** (*see*). Talleyrand later opposed the sale of French territory in North America to the United States in 1803, but **Napoleon** (*see*) ignored his advice (*see* **Louisiana Purchase**). Born of a noble Parisian family, Talleyrand was educated to be a priest. He rose to the position of bishop of Autun, but in 1791 he left the Roman Catholic Church to work in the French government. Talleyrand's talent for political survival has rarely been equaled. He served under Louis XVI (1754–1793), under the Directory during the **French Revolution** (*see*), under Napoleon, and again under

Charles Maurice de Talleyrand

the monarchy when the Bourbons were restored in 1814. Despite his opportunism and taste for diplomatic intrigue, Talleyrand advocated constitutional liberty, and his contributions to the cause of European peace were of the utmost importance.

TECUMSEH (1768?–1813). This Shawnee chief organized an Indian confederacy of 32 tribes that threatened to halt American migration to the Western frontier. Tecumseh, who lived with his brother **Tenskwatawa** (*see*) near the Tippecanoe River in present-day Indiana, believed that Indian territory belonged to all tribes in common and that no one tribe or chieftain had the right to cede or sell land. He undertook to form a single powerful confederacy of Indian tribes from the Old Northwest, the South, and the Mississippi Valley to prevent further encroachment by white men. While Tecumseh was away recruiting members for his league in 1811, he left Tenskwatawa, who was known as the Prophet, in charge of the Tippecanoe settlement. On No-

vember 7, 1811, Tenskwatawa attacked an American army sent out under William Henry Harrison (1773–1841) to break up the confederation. The Indians sustained heavy losses, and their league was destroyed. At the beginning of the War of 1812, Tecumseh and his followers migrated to Canada and joined the British. He was commissioned a brigadier general and took part in the capture of Detroit. In 1813, the Americans forced the British and their Indian allies to retreat into Canada. Tecumseh was subsequently killed by American forces under Harrison at the Battle of Thames in central Ontario on October 5, 1813. His death ended the Indian alliance with England, thus securing the Northwestern frontier for the United States.

Tecumseh

TENSKWATAWA (1768?–1834). Known as the Prophet, Tenskwatawa was the brother of the Shawnee chieftain **Tecumseh** (*see*). About 1805, Tenskwatawa fell into a trance in which he saw heavenly visions, and thereafter he devoted himself to religious

activity. He acquired a large following by predicting an eclipse of the sun in 1806. Tenskwatawa supported Tecumseh's efforts to establish an Indian confederation. In 1811, while Tecumseh was away, he was left in charge of the Indian encampment at Tippecanoe, in present-day Indiana. Despite Tecumseh's warning not to fight, Tenskwatawa attacked an American army under William Henry Harrison (1773–1841), who had been sent to break up the confederation. The Indians—who Tenskwatawa had prophesied would defeat the Americans—suffered heavy losses, and Tenskwatawa lost most of his prestige. He refused to participate in the War of 1812 and moved to Canada, where he lived on a British pension until 1826, when he returned to the United States.

TOMPKINS, Daniel D. (1774–1825). As governor of New York (1807–1817), Tompkins proposed a number of reforms, including the abolition of slavery in the state. As a result of his efforts, slavery was finally abolished in New York State in 1827. Tompkins, a lawyer, was active in state politics before serving as an associate justice of the New York supreme court (1804–1807). He left the court upon winning election as governor. Tompkins served as commander in chief of the New York militia during the War of 1812. He was twice elected Vice-President (1817–1825) under **James Monroe** (*see*), but he was often absent from his post because of excessive drinking.

TREATY OF MORFONTAINE. *See* **Convention of 1800.**

TREATY OF SAN ILDEFONSO. *See* **Charles IV.**

TRIPOLITAN WAR. *See* **Barbary Wars.**

TRUMBULL, John (1750–1831). Trumbull, an American poet, was born in Connecticut. He passed the Yale entrance examinations at the age of seven but did not attend the college until he was 13. In 1772, he composed his first important work, a 1,700-line poem about college education called *The Progress of Dulness.* In 1773, Trumbull moved to Boston to study law under **John Adams** (*see*). Two years later he started writing *M'Fingal,* his most famous poem. Published in 1782, it was a satiric attack on British military leaders during the Revolution. The poem was a popular success and was reprinted more than 30 times between 1782 and 1840. After *M'Fingal* was published, Trumbull abandoned poetry for politics. He was a judge of the Connecticut superior court (1801–1819) and of the supreme court of errors (1808–1819). He was a cousin of the painter John Trumbull (1756–1843).

V

VIRGINIA PLAN. The Virginia Plan, which was drafted by **James Madison** (*see*), was presented to the Constitutional Convention on May 29, 1787, by **Edmund Randolph** (*see*). The plan proposed a federal government consisting of a judiciary, a two-chamber legislature, and an executive chosen by the legislature. Because each state was to be represented in the legislature according to its population, this plan would have been advantageous to the larger states. The plan also proposed a revisory council composed of the executive and representatives from the judi-

ciary. This council would have veto power over the legislative acts. The Virginia Plan was opposed by the smaller states, which supported the **New Jersey Plan** (*see*). The **Connecticut Compromise** (*see*) of July 16, 1787, provided a satisfactory solution by granting the states equal representation in the Senate and representation according to population in the House of Representatives.

W

WASHINGTON, D.C. Construction was begun in 1792 on Washington, D.C., the capital of the United States. Eight years later, the federal government moved its headquarters there from Philadelphia. The **Constitution** (*see*) provided for a federal district that would, "by Cession of particular States, and the acceptance of Congress, become the Seat of Government of the United States." To avoid state interference in the district's affairs, Congress was given exclusive legislative powers to govern the new capital. The decision to locate the city on the Potomac River was made by Congress in July, 1790, as a result of a political compromise between **Alexander Hamilton** of New York and **James Madison** and **Thomas Jefferson** of Virginia (*see all*). The two Virginians agreed to support Hamilton's financial policies if he would support the Southern plan to build the capital on the Potomac. **George Washington** (*see*) chose the actual site and appointed **Pierre Charles L'Enfant** (*see*) to design the city. The original federal district covered an area of 100 square miles and included Georgetown, which was ceded by Maryland, and Alexandria, which was ceded by Virginia.

In 1791, the area was named the Territory of Columbia, and the city was named in honor of Washington. By 1796, the area was informally known as the District of Columbia. At the request of its residents, Alexandria was returned to Virginia in 1847. When Georgetown became part of the city proper in 1895, the District of Columbia and Washington became one and the same. Washington was formerly governed by three commissioners appointed by the President. Since 1974, Washingtonians have elected their own mayor and city council. They also elect one non-voting member of the U.S. House of Representatives.

WASHINGTON, George (*Continued from Volume 3*). When the Revolution ended in 1783, Washington hoped to retire "from all public engagements" to tend his estate at **Mount Vernon** (*see*). In 1785, however, he was host there to delegates from Virginia and Maryland, who met to regulate navigation on the Potomac. The following year, he attended the Annapolis Convention, which was an attempt to reach agreement on matters of interstate commerce. It had become clear to Washington that the Articles of Confederation, which had gone into effect in March, 1781, were too weak to govern the states effectively. He supported proposals for a stronger national charter. When the Constitutional Convention opened in Philadelphia on May 25, 1787, Washington was chosen to preside. He gave his wholehearted support to the **Constitution** (*see*), which went into effect on March 4, 1789. Chosen unanimously as the first President, Washington took office in New York on April 30, 1789. He had to borrow money to pay his travel expenses to New

York for the inauguration. Washington's first term of office was a relatively calm one. Striving for national unity, he appointed a conservative, **Alexander Hamilton** (*see*), as Secretary of the Treasury, and a liberal, **Thomas Jefferson** (*see*), as Secretary of State. He traveled throughout the young nation to confer with regional leaders and enlist their support for the central government. Washington sought to remain above partisan politics, but his basic conservatism soon became evident. He increasingly supported the Federalist policies advocated by Hamilton. He was unanimously reelected President in 1793, but his second term was a period of heated controversy. His support of Hamilton's stand on the excise tax and the national bank aroused the bitter opposition of Jeffersonians, as did his refusal to honor the military alliance with France signed in 1778. Disturbed by the political excesses of the **French Revolution** (*see*) and France's declaration of war on England, he issued a proclamation of neutrality in 1793. The **Whiskey Rebellion** (*see*), which involved farmers in rural Pennsylvania, was suppressed in 1794 without any loss of life, but much bitterness resulted. Many were angered by **Jay's Treaty** (*see*) of 1794, which granted numerous concessions to England and got few in return. Washington tried in vain to prevent the party rivalry between Hamilton's Federalists and Jefferson's Democratic-Republicans. On the positive side, the victory of General Anthony Wayne (1745–1796) at the Battle of **Fallen Timbers** (*see*) in 1794 eased the government's problems with hostile Indians in the Northwest Territory, north of the Ohio River, and a treaty with Spain in 1795 established good relations

Two years before his death, Washington was sketched by Benjamin Latrobe.

between the two nations. Still, Washington was irritated by political attacks branding him an aristocrat and an enemy of democracy. Weary of public life, he declined to run for a third term. In his final speech (*see* **Washington's Farewell Address**), he warned the nation against "permanent alliances" with foreign powers, "the fury of party spirit," and "the impostures of pretended patriotism." He retired on March 3, 1797. When war with France threatened in 1798, President **John Adams** (*see*) appointed Washington commander in chief of the army. However, war was averted, and he never served. Washington fell ill while inspecting his estate on December 12, 1799. Before his death two days later, he said, "I die hard, but I am not afraid to go." He was buried at Mount Vernon. Washington is revered as the Father of his Country, and his birthday in February is a national holiday.

WASHINGTON'S FAREWELL ADDRESS.

In 1796, at the end of his second term as President, **George Washington** (*see*) decided to retire from public life. He drafted his Farewell Address as a final statement of his years as President. Published in the Philadelphia newspapers on September 18, 1796, the address stressed the necessity of a strong national government. Washington warned against the establishment of political parties, which he believed were trying to assume political power for personal ends. He spoke of the necessity of education and morality, and he urged impartial justice toward all nations. However, Washington discouraged any foreign entanglements, saying "there can be no greater error than to expect or calculate upon real favors from nation to nation." He closed his address with the hope that his statements would "recur to moderate the fury of party spirit, to warn against the mischiefs of foreign intrigue, to guard against the impostures of pretended patriotism."

WEBSTER, Noah

(1758–1843). A lawyer and a schoolteacher, Webster is best known for writing *An American Dictionary of the English Language,* published in 1828. He first became an important figure in American education in the 1780s, with the publication of the first American reader, a grammar, and a speller that was known informally as The Blue-backed Speller. Largely because of his efforts, a federal copyright law was passed in 1790. He also helped to establish Amherst College in 1821. Webster worked almost 20 years gathering words and definitions for his dictionary to give it a distinctive American flavor. Much of his life was spent working on a revised edition.

WHISKEY REBELLION.

In 1791, Congress passed an excise tax on distilled liquors and ordered that offenders be tried in federal courts. Objections to the tax were especially strong in the Monongahela Valley in western Pennsylvania, where many farmers derived much of their income from the distillation of corn. In addition, there was already much antagonism among frontiersmen toward the growing power of the federal government. In 1794, the tax collectors began to meet with violent resistance. When the governor of Pennsylvania refused to enforce collections, President **George Washington** (*see*), at the urging of Secretary of the Treasury **Alexander Hamilton** (*see*), mobilized about 13,000 militia from surrounding states to suppress the defiant farmers. Hamilton and Henry "Light Horse Harry" Lee (1756–1818) then led a march into the insurgent counties, quickly crushing all opposition. Although those arrested were later pardoned by Washington, hatred toward the President's Federalist followers remained for many years. Resistance to the whiskey tax was never a full-scale rebellion. Some historians believe that Hamilton overdramatized the incident as an excuse to assert forcibly the authority of the federal government.

WILSON, Alexander (1766–1813). Born in Scotland, Wilson came to America in 1794. He taught school and began a study of birds that resulted in the publication of his 13-volume classic, *American Ornithology*, although it was not completed until 20 years after his death. It was the earliest work of its type to appear in any branch of science in America.

WINDER, William Henry (1775–1824). Winder, whose military incompetence allowed the British to capture and burn the nation's capital, was a prominent Balti-

more lawyer before he entered the army at the outset of the War of 1812. He became a brigadier general the following year and was commander of the Potomac District at the Battle of Bladensburg, Maryland, on August 24, 1814. Although the poorly trained militiamen led by Winder had the more advantageous position, they scattered as soon as the British attacked. This allowed the enemy to march unopposed on Washington, D.C. By the following morning, the capital was in British hands, and its major buildings were being burned. The extent of Winder's responsibility for the disaster has been debated ever since. He left the army the following year and resumed his law practice.

XYZ

XYZ AFFAIR. American relations with France deteriorated seriously after **Jay's Treaty** (*see*) with Britain in 1794, which the French government believed violated the French-American alliance of 1778. The French retaliated by intercepting American ships. In 1797, President **John Adams** (*see*) sent **Charles Cotesworth Pinckney, Elbridge Gerry** (*see both*), and John Marshall (1755–1835) to Paris to negotiate a settlement. However, the French foreign minister, **Talleyrand** (*see*), refused to receive the Americans. Instead, he designated three unofficial agents to negotiate with them. These agents—who became known as X, Y, and Z—demanded that America pay for alleged wrongs done to France and not only grant a large loan to finance the French war with Britain but also pay a bribe of about $240,000 to Talleyrand. The United States envoys refused the terms, and Adams made public the attempted blackmail. The XYZ Affair resulted in tense bitterness on both sides and led to undeclared naval warfare between the two nations for several years.

FRANKLIN DELANO ROOSEVELT LIBRARY

An armed American merchantman beats off a French privateer in 1799 in the undeclared naval war that broke out between the United States and France.